AMAZE SIN GRACE

BY

TESLIM JOHNSON

Voice Of Teslim Ministry

Agape Behaviour Publishing

Proverbs chapter 23 verse 7
"As a man think in his heart, that is what he is"

CONTENTS

CHAPTERS

CONTENTS

PREACH PREACHER

PRAY

I wanna pray

I wanna pray for purpose, broken lives

And curses

I wanna pray

I wanna pray about the society, the twisted screwed up mentalities, the narrow minded human beings, the bent up chewed up realities

I wanna pray
I wanna pray for the human race, how we want everything in haste

I wanna pray

I wanna pray about certain atmospheres

Certain things that wear and tear

Lack of faith and dreamless peers

I wanna pray

I wanna pray about immorality and those distributing profanity

Filthy acts like that and companies promoting it and thinking it is normal and that

I wanna pray

I wanna pray for God's presence

God's forgiveness, patience and reverence

I wanna pray

I wanna pray for the nation every race and denomination

I wanna pray

Amaze Sin Grace

I just wanna pray, I wanna pray for the kids, the adults, the teachers, the drug dealers, leaders, the government, cults and gangs

I wanna pray

I wanna pray to someone who will let me pray someone who can feel my pain, someone that don't seem lame, someone that don't act fake or vain

I wanna pray

I wanna pray for vision, the fruits of the Holy Spirit and wisdom

I wanna pray

I wanna pray to the world and talk about the lack unity and talk about pulling together to try to make things better

I wanna pray

I'm not finished I wanna pray, I just wanna pray

To whom it may concern I wanna pray

I wanna pray

I wanna pray to people who do things for self gain and like to watch people feel the pain and strain

I wanna pray

I wanna pray about people with lack of vision also peeps causing division

I wanna pray

I wanna pray about humans thinking wrong is right and thinking the dark is light

I wanna pray

I wanna pray coz divine purpose lives inside of you

Do you wanna pray?

Coz I wanna pray!

INTRO

On a mission to find peace and God!

One night I was out with my friends, Eddie, Sachel and Ryan, and I must have started beating up a Pizza Hut delivery driver near by and revved his motorbike engine coz I wanted the Pizza he was delivering, but he did not want to give it to me.

So I was just making trouble unnecessarily, "I was on rowdy mode", silly, I got the pizza in the end, coz he ran off. Instead of eating it, I just threw it like a mad man? Eddie was not going to take me to the BBQ anymore and started shaking his head saying he weren't taking me to his friend's Jenny's BBQ, but I insisted and insisted I was calming down! Somehow we made our way to the BBQ, and I met Curtis, Million, Jenny, Charlotte and Tope at Jenny's BBQ. I was so drunk that night and it was as if these guys disabled my drunkenness, by truly ministering to me with love.

I believe now there was strong positive vibes, peace and joy that it over powered my drunken state! I could relate to Curtis, I felt he was real, maybe coz he had a gold teeth as well and he seemed my age and seem to have been where I had been, and we just clicked straight away! I went clubbing that night after the BBQ and agreed to follow Curtis to church the next day. The thing is, I have always been a man of my word, and so if I say I would do something, I always would.

I came back from clubbing about [7.30a.m] and heard a beep outside my window about [10.15a.m], I looked out the window tired, and to my surprise I saw Curtis, I thought is he for real? So I jumped in the toilet washed my teeth and jumped into his car with the same clothes I clubbed with, which was smelling of smoke and I went to church.

I had a hard, hang over, and when I got to the church I was sleepy throughout the whole service but the place seemed cool, there were loads of beautiful ladies there, and loads of youth it seemed to be kosher so I just relaxed. Then near the end this Pastor called Brian Houston, from a church called Hill song in Australia, gave an alter call, asking people who wanted to give their lives to Christ and get salvation or re dedicate their lives back to God, should come forward.

He said: "there are many of you in here today who want to be made whole", right there and then the Holy Spirit was knocking on the door to my heart, I felt this man of God was talking to me and I wanted to be made whole! What did I have to lose?

I had tried everything in search for a peace and lived my life to the max. All the money I made, the girls I slept with, the cars, gold, drugs, alcohol, partying was not enough it was temporary peace and joy. I suddenly remembered reading in the Bible once "In God is fullness of joy", that's what I needed forever the fullness of that joy. I started to have a strong pull "right there" the Spirit was drawing me, my heart was beating faster, but I was trying to avoid it suddenly my foot just walked, not me? "It come like" someone was using a remote control, to direct me forward. I was like what am I doing? There I was being set free for good! I closed my eyes cried and said the salvation prayer and got hold of God again!

What if Eddie hadn't taken me or avoided going to the BBQ?

What if? I don't think I would be writing this book?

APPRECIATION

I was Amazed in Sin then I found something greater which was 'Grace!'

This book God led me to write is for the Glory of God Jesus Christ The Alpha and Omega. To encourage and relate for the believers, unbelievers, righteous, the different races, faces, the whole hearted, broken hearted, the backslider, the painful, the faithful, the Anointed one that fears God Almighty, the strugglers and hustlers, the upright, the discouraged, the poor, the rich, the strong, the weak, the sinner, the one that is lost, the one that is found, and last but not least the true and diligent server. I had to get this book out by any means necessary I have a lot to say and share.

Father in the name of mighty Jesus I pray that your power and might and Holy Spirit will guide and help the restless person, that your Words and your commandments will be exalted and done in the name of Jesus Amen.

Besides God Almighty these people have inspired me and have let God use them as a tool to have an impact in my life.

My dearest and beloved mother and father.

My baby my lady my love my wife Yvonne K.F.Johnson, my mentor and good friend Mark Powell, a true friend Curtis Gabriel, Darren Lee Joseph, Aundrea Nyle, Jenny Beharry, Byron Clarke, Susan Reid, Tracy Anderson, Patricia Brackenridge, Marcia Daley, Brian Daley, Susan Harriott, Aunty Dami, Janet, John Dayo Adeagbo, Lynval Sydney, Jeff "Que Pasa" Mano! Righteous Crew, M.O.D: Efrem Buckle (E.Miner) and wife, Patrick (Triple.P) and wife, Robert Prendergast (Pilgrim) and wife, Andrew Williams - Calvary Chapel, Charlotte, Hafis Joel Raji, Pastor Ian Christensen, Dennise Christensen, Emmanuel Akpata, Angela Akpata, Pastor Alwyn Wall and wife, Rev Roy Smith, Pastor Brian Houston, and many more I am eternally grateful and thank God for their lives and influences.

"Big Up!

Before you get into my life, firstly, I'd just like to share something with you!

"I have a confession to make", I really do not like reading, I dislike reading,

I always used to enjoy reading cartoon comics or things with pictures in it or I wouldn't be motivated, *"no wonder I messed up in secondary school"*. Mind you though, I have to read and more importantly, reading the Bible, it's my spiritual food and a must. It's the only thing I study seriously. I don't even take the newspapers or the news seriously, but the Holy Bible it has to be done or there wouldn't be any point being a Christian.

Secondly, I would like to sincerely apologise to anyone in the past that I have ever scammed, robbed, beat up, had beaten up, abused, I am sorry.

I want you to understand this book thoroughly remembering where God has brought me from, and encourage you with deep scriptures and teachings in the Bible that changed my life and that can also change your life, so make sure you read those scriptures in that book the Holy Bible it's deep!

Sometimes I hear that famous Christian saying: since I turned Christian I've never looked back, well in fact that ain't right we all look back at times but we will not turn back. Coz when you get to know God and fear Him and take time to have a relationship with Him you start knowing you are held accountable for what you know!

FOREWORD

The Book

Amaze Sin Grace by Teslim Johnson who shares his real life experiences in this very therapeutic transparent book!

Teslim Johnson shares his struggles as a youth, his abuse, his journey from a Muslim to Christian, from a criminal to a Christian, bizarre sightings and visions, breaking habits, convictions!
A 'Profound dynamic book' very relevant for this generation!

I was lead to write this book purely by the influence of the 'Holy Spirit' Everybody is searching for knowledge! I found it so can you! "Can I get a Amen!"

To show you I can't make it without God! That we all need God!

Church is fellowship, a place of unity, a place of love, a place of worship and a hospital where people who need healing can come and be healed.

The purpose of this book is for the Word and knowledge of Jesus Christ to be spread and used as a Bible reference, Evangelising tool for the:

Community, Media, Society, Streets

Youth centers, Detention centers

Prison ministry

Christians, Non-Christians

My generation and the generation to come

Our Reality and Our Youth.

I am confident this book will change a negative mindset. To the criminal, to the violent, the drug dealer messing up innocent lives, to the greedy, the needy, the abuser, the homosexual, the paedophile, the rich and the poor, the sick, the disabled! Whatever walk of life you are from you 'know' who you are!

'YOU CAN BE SET FREE'...

A friend once encouraged me, at a time when I felt down in the New Year of 2004, she said: whatever it is it can't be so bad, life is 'good', and life does have something to offer, it's the New Year and you must decide what you want and make choices.

Fix your mentality and mindset, you do not have anything to prove to anyone but yourself!

There are two types of people in this world 'winners' and 'losers', 'winners' hold on, if you fall get back up!   You have to be a 'winner'. "I guess that's what I'm saying to the world!"

"Be a 'winner' with Christ Jesus!"

I would specially like to thank Tracey Robinson for proof reading this book for me and by being sensitive to the Holy Spirit to help me make this book and vision happen!

God Bless You

Why?

Writing a book had to be done, I was truly led by the Holy Spirit of God.

I have learnt to lean on Him, have a relationship with Him, talk with Him, dwell in His presence and I suppose it's another way of also sharing my testimony, and more importantly, giving something back to God.

"Because I used to be known, and labelled as a crooked person one of the best thieves, scammers, a money person, designer kid, incognito, a.k.a, for those out there, maybe friends or people that know of me, this book is not another making money scheme, "for your information! *Cut a brother some slack,* "I'm being extremely serious here".

A lot of people are gonna read my book and are gonna be shocked at the things I have been up to in my life, especially my mother and father, I celebrate all those people who just thought of me as just a nice young man with manners, not knowing the things I really got up to." Bless God" for you!

I have to share and reach out to you guys out there, in my own words and explain about what I have experienced out there!

Whatever age, race, colour, or profession you belong to.

Where Am I Coming From?

I had a street mentality. Some of the phrases I use are how we speak on road, as a young black Londoner in different lingo and slang, which a lot of people relate with, and a reflection of how I used to speak.

"I actually remember when I gave my testimony in church, I added I would like to be able to speak proper English through out my personal life".

I can actually see I'm getting better though, not just trying to put on the well-spoken act, by trying to talk properly in just job interviews.

I am also coming from an analytical side to clarify understanding straight away, by giving you a revelation of what has been revealed to me as I've got to know the mind of God. Examples of phrases like 'The Holy Bible' which is 'The Mind Of God', and 'Christians' which is 'Christ Like People' and other phrases that I keep highlighting.

I didn't have a revelation before of the knowledge and understanding of what the 'Bible' really was or what a 'Christian' is but now I know. I want you to also know and digest this revelation. So don't get confused by the repetitiveness of the meaning of certain words and points I put in brackets.

Those of you that think you are the only ones that went through stuff and burdening yourself with that thought that no one knows about your circumstances, trials, issues and all that jazz. And that you've done too much bad things for God to forgive you, or even killed someone. I'm gonna break it down for you, to the young and old brethren and brethreness especially the youths.

God Almighty will forgive you if you *'openly'* confess your sins and accept Him!

Accept Jesus Christ in your life, and serve Him in spirit and in truth. *"Yeah, ya better believe it!* "Oh man, God is such a merciful God!!!

This book is designed to stir and exercise your spirit. So make sure when you're reading don't be one of those lazy Christians or non-Christians, who can't be bothered to pick up their Bible (God's Mind) and check out scriptures. This book ain't gonna write all the scriptures down. Don't forget we live by the *WORD!*

No one can know too much, even if you know common scriptures, the word needs to soak into your spirit and come alive and create a "divine" understanding, our minds have to be renewed daily *"know what I'm talking about?*

Just be blessed by what is on these pieces of paper.

I'm gonna tell it like it is! Popping in and out of chapters like God did in the 'Old' and 'New' Testament, in the Bible (The Mind of God)

CAN YOU HANDLE THE TRUTH?

"Now writing a book at the age of 23 is a big fat testimony the patients and guidance by the Holy Spirit has been phenomenal, coz boy I'm an impatient person, ask my mum she will tell you that I always rush and want and do things quick, quick, *"You are too inquisitive"* as she always says.

"I suppose it's just the art of being a doer and believe me, I am a doer! What ever I wanna do, I do. *'Trust me'*.

Please get your Bible (God's Mind) as you read this book!

"Oh yeah ladies and all races don't get offended or upset coz of certain terms like bro and stuff, coz it's 'a figure of speech' a lot of my words are slang I'm referring to every creature on earth! So don't feel left out cool, we have an understanding!

When you're done reading this book, you need to apply the Word to your life, coz nothing will change unless you apply the Word of God to your life.

MY TESTIMONY

Chapter 1

Colourful Life Begins

Touch down on earth *September 13ᵗʰ 1978.*

Born in South London, stayed in Battersea South London, and then taken to Nigeria at the age of three where my life started. "Well actually I remember life from age six.

"Well I guess you want to know my background, it's itching you init?

"Well I am from a very strict and loving family!

I was brought up, I guess to the best of parenthood my parents knew, although that's not what I used to think at the time.

God I saw and learnt a lot of things in Nigeria!

Anyways at the age of six I would do everything for myself, I was an independent youngster. I had to be, because I was the first born and 'thee man' or you could say soon to be the second man of the house, although before my mum met my dad she had a girl and before my dad met my mum he had a girl. So I had two half sisters who were older but none of them lived with us and to tell you the truth I didn't know where any of them were? I do remember seeing my half sister from my mum's side at my grandmother's house now and again.

I remember back in the days my mother and father would always be at work, I must say my mother and father were hard workers they weren't no *"Mickey Mouse"* workers they worked really hard. As a matter of fact they still do.

My parents were well educated too, my father used to study in London and Germany so he could speak a bit of German and had various other qualifications.

In Nigeria my father was always at work and always seemed to be tired and vex. Everytime he got home he seemed vex? I did not know where he was working then, but now know, he was working at a petrol station no wonder he was vex, coz he wasn't using his full abilities and potential, that job thinking about it must have been a boring job.

My mum owned and ran a busy restaurant with my aunty, her younger sister, where I used to hang out sometimes and help out when I was taken there, which was exciting to me, coz I met different people and I used to just chill out really.

I remember meeting a friendly police officer once at my mum's restaurant that was talking to me and telling me jokes and he even let me hold his rifle, it was a big, long, heavy gun. I remember pointing it at a tree and I was very, very, very tempted to pull 'that trigger', just to see the damage it would do and hear the sound it would make!

I didn't though coz I knew if I did that, the police officer would have given me one hot backhand and beat me. One, beat me coz he was older and two, beat me because it would have been disrespect and I knew that so I didn't.

Whether my parents were at home or not I had to make sure the house was clean, and my home work was done, and make sure my English and maths were in tact, it was like a routine that was a must do thing like going to school.

At school we had to be smart and speak well. We all were well spoken in fluent English, looking back at that memory I used to speak posh 'man'.

I was always constantly taught how to behave and particularly to be respectful.

When my mother or father got back from either work, or whenever I was among adults I had to automatically say welcome sir or ma and take any bag or shopping or anything that was carried by anyone older than me into the house or else!

I would say my parents were just a little too strict on me. Looking back particularly at my father he always had an expectancy! I was always expected to be smarter than other people my age or compared to other kids, thought to have been smart by my parents, which was something I hated and would sometimes affect my confidence, and the main reason I sometimes was told why I never got pocket money.

I was told I never deserved it or earned it, but I just thought it was excuses and my dad being too strict with me. I feel I was under a lot of pressure, which I could not handle as a child, and as a teenager growing up, which some what destroyed me.

"Being told to be the best, be smart and work hard was good and bad, in the sense of it had its advantages and disadvantages.

My main concern was always hoping I didn't get beaten or my teacher wouldn't beat me or tell my parents bad things about me.

My God, when I was little till I was about seventeen I got whooped!

Teslim has been through the belt, backhand, cane, whip, slipper, wire, wood, pot it's funny and not funny!

I remember like it was yesterday when I was in school and I asked the teacher to go to the toilet in the middle of an English lesson. You really and truly have got to have courage to ask the teacher that sort of thing during a lesson, but I was very, very desperate at the time. I would have done it where I was sitting if I didn't go which would have been embarrassing.

Anyways, I put my hand up whilst the teacher was teaching and I started shaking whilst I proceeded to walk towards my tutor and I stood there quietly practically stuttering begging my tutor to go to the toilet. I think she thought I just wanted a break or something coz she did not take me serious at all and sent me back to my seat?

So I went back to my seat but did not sit down, I pleaded: "please ma, please. She kept her back to me as she was writing on the black board, then as I was begging my whole body and speech was straining and tightening up I could not hold it any longer, coz I was so desperate to go to the toilet!

The embarrassment happened'. Out of the blue it just came out? I let loose I couldn't hold it, *'I started to urinate in my shorts'*, my bottom half looked like a hosepipe flowing with yellow water pouring out. I remember making a puddle and looking down at it in relief, but not being able to stop peeing, then looking up stiff and frozen like a statue, at a 'terror' *"yep"* my tutor! Who was standing up wondering what I was standing and looking at, then to her amazement finding out I was urinating on the floor.........

The whole class was looking straight ahead and fighting not to burst out laughing, everyone in that classroom was looking forward with their eyes wedged to the corner, looking at the action that was about to take place with the teacher and me.

As urine dripped from my shorts onto the floor, her floor, her classroom, the noise of the dripping urine got louder, it sounded like a tap bouncing off concrete.

She was shocked, so shocked she stood there watching until I finished dripping, then *'she went for me'*, and started chasing me around the classroom, nearly slipping in my urine. She then grabbed a thick cane out her of her variety of canes and I managed to open the door and ran out of the classroom. She chased me catching me a few times but I kept slipping out of her hands. Then I got to the boys toilets and locked myself inside.

It was one of those open top toilets, I was crouching down looking up in fear and irritation with the sticky urine all over my socks and uniform, and then I saw her face over me with one long hand waving a thick cane! She tried to hit me, but she couldn't reach me so she finally gave up, she couldn't be bothered to climb in.

I believe if she had caught me, I reckon she wouldn't have really beaten me, I reckon she would have *'killed me'* with her bear hands.

An hour later she came back to the toilet and I was persuaded by two other teachers to come out of the toilet so I finally unlocked the toilet, after the teachers assured me I wouldn't be beaten or the headmaster told of what happened, as long as I came out of the toilet and cleaned and moped the classroom and four other class rooms, before I went home. You didn't get any cleaners in that school, the school children did it.

When I finally got the guts to come out of the toilet I was happy and relieved to see that my teacher never had a cane in her hand, but she looked at me in disgust then she dragged me back to the classroom by my ears!

Little did I know she had somehow told my mum what I did so when I got home that evening I got a hot slap, thank the lord it was only my mum who knew about what happened. *Phew!!!!!!!!*

Chapter 2

Kid Dilemmas

I remember another dilemma at school back in Nigeria, the whole class had to line up including me, for the teacher to give us our beats with the cane. The beats were equivalent to how many answers we all individually got wrong, in other words queuing up for a whooping! *"Guess who by?*

" Yep you guessed it! "The same teacher who nearly killed me!

Coz most of us didn't get our maths homework right, we were being taught a lesson. Some kids were fortunate, I saw some walk off with one strike, meanwhile I was in the line watching kids scream as they were getting hit on their back, legs, arms and backside coz they would not take the punishment properly.

"The teacher wanted to connect! Trust me!

A lot of the kids were still backing off and getting scared of getting their 'punishment' the fortunate ones were the ones that got one or two things wrong which meant one or two strikes with the cane. Unlike the others not wanting to go next coz they had about twelve wrong and I was among those which equalled twelve smacks.

The way the teacher was whipping everyone with that cane, seemed like she was letting out all her frustration. *"Don't think some kids didn't try to run, they did* but, the teacher was smart she locked the door and those kids that did try, felt it more.

I was also one of them that felt it more, don't forget we are in a hot country and all we had on were two white socks, shorts and a hollow short sleeve shirt meanwhile the teacher had four varieties of canes. 'A long cane', 'a thin cane', 'a thick cane,' and 'a rigid cane'.

It's funny come to think about it now, the teacher would send three of us out sometimes to go and pick the finest, freshest canes from the yard, when she wanted a fresh set of these bamboo sticks.

The thick and rigid ones, I didn't mind so much, because the teachers knew where to draw the line with those and of course they could really hurt someone.

We were only little six and seven year olds and it would be a bit dangerous, but the thin ones, my, my, my I can remember feeling the pain, it felt like thousands of stinging nettles stuffed down your backside, it's similar to the sting of someone flicking thousands of elastic bands on your backside or being whipped with a wire.

Those thin canes were the worst, you felt that pain and it stung for a good two weeks.

I should know, I felt all four canes and my mother has dealt with me with a wire in the past. Yep a certain predicament one time, actually it was my brother and I but I won't go into that story, it hurt man it's tough being a man believe.

I suppose beating had some effect on certain kids to learn and be sharp but me nope it never helped me.

I remember witnessing a kid getting beats by the headmaster that is something you have to avoid coz if it gets to the headmaster that is it!

At the tender age of seven I loved playing with friends, I always used to love play fighting and real fighting with kids. I also used to be quite creative, I would make paper toys including aeroplanes, kites, and bows and arrows out of broomsticks and cello tape when I could find any, that was. The only time I got to do that, was when my parents were out, or when I was with my cousins or at school so I guess that's why I always used to sneak out, most of the time I would unfortunately get caught, and would get the cane!

So as you can see I was very limited to how much play I was allowed.

I remember having to read my times tables out to my father once. I had to do some maths homework and my father was always waiting to see my finished homework.

Most of the time I would get a few wrong and would get my hand hit with the cane about ten times.

I would somehow, get some more right then I would be left alone, and told I didn't know anything and that I was an idiot and I had to go and learn.

I remember one weekend my father set me some homework to do the night before and that Saturday I wanted to play out and walk around. My parents were out so I thought ok an opportunity, so the first thing I did was look for some money in my fathers room, I found some and took it and set off.

I went to the market I bought a new pair of slippers and some chewing gum and just took a long walk, then bumped into some boys who were making a nice big kite. So I asked to help and played with them. Whilst I was out I lost track of the time plus I hadn't done my homework or washed the plates or swept the floor and about five hours later when I finally got back home I realised I shut the door behind me and didn't have a key I also realised my homework and house work wasn't done then I realised how long I had been out.

I thought ok let me check if my father's car is around and to my shock it was back that meant big, big trouble!!

Anyway I built up my confidence hid the slippers I bought and spat the chewing gum out then I headed for the door which was wide open, my heart was "over pounding". I crept in and went into the living room, saw my father said hello he said: "where have you been" and started shouting, all I could say was sorry sir sorry but he headed for the door and started to bolt up the door. I realised then I was going to get the biggest hiding ever in my entire life and I looked everywhere I could quickly run to, to get out of the house but there was only one way out it was the front door.

Now this was the first and last time I saw my father pull out a real whip and head towards me. I looked in shock and was crying saying sorry then he said: "come here", I started to make a run for it, my father chased me all over the living room into the toilets where I locked myself in. Unfortunately, the toilets we had in our home were open top ones so my father proceeded to climb over. As soon as I saw his face I unlocked the toilet ran to the door it was bolted and there was no way on earth I was getting the front door open so I ran to the balcony, the doors were open so I ran out into our small balcony and shouted screaming and shouting my father is going to kill me.

People started coming out and shouting up to my father: "please don't beat him", but it didn't help, my father grabbed me even before I could think of jumping the high balcony. It was over in about five minutes, I really did get the beating of my lifetime, my father had found out about the money and dirty dishes and all the rest of it.

My arms, back, legs, hands and especially my bottom was in pain! I got a good hiding my father kept on saying he has never been a thief and I am a thief, he never taught me to steal so I will learn a lesson, and if he ever caught me stealing again, he will mark my hands.

As a kid I had many desires, I wanted things such as toys sweets and money.

I did not see my mother and father much, because most of their time was spent at work but the relationship I had with my parents, was very clear, I always had full respect for my mother and father. If I did anything wrong, such as forgetting to sweep the floor, clean or wash something or forget certain manners, I would get a hot slap, back hand, the cane or the slipper, so as you can see I was very disciplined as a young man. I always had to address my mother as Ma my father as Sir and anyone older than me as aunty or uncle. I could not forget my manners at home, at school, with my uncles and aunties, or anyone who were at least two years older than me, otherwise they would automatically be authorised to give me a beating with the cane and I would get seconds from my Father.

Well you would have thought being aware of all this knowledge I would have been perfect, the answer is no I wasn't, I always managed to lose focus to play and think about money, toys and girls.

I would continue to steal money and things from the shop because I had no money,

I desired sweets and toys. I always liked nice things that I got very little of, despite the discipline and always getting caught stealing. Personally at the time, it was an act that I was good at and I found I got most of the things I wanted, plus it was fun. I guess most of these influences were from the television and seeing other kids with what I wanted, but didn't have.

This act also had a huge impact on my life leading me to my first arrest when I was fourteen and over fifteen arrests after that till I was twenty-two years old. I guess no one ever helped me to go about it the right way, the problem was never dealt with properly, it was always bypassed, and just unacceptable.

Chapter 3

Exposed To Sex And Lust

You would have thought I would have been your average seven year old that just loved making toys and playing with toys this was not the case.

My child hood changed at that age.

When I was seven I was sexually abused. It was by a fifteen-year-old young woman who used to baby-sit my brother and myself sometimes, whilst my mother and father were at work and on holiday periods. She had full sex with my brother and me. I couldn't fully penetrate but I remember having a soft erection. My parents were not aware of this at all, when they read this book they will be.

Looking back on this I realised it was an act which I did not do of my own free will. It broke my innocence and corrupted me, and had an influence on me, which led me to corrupt other young girls of my age leading to more sexual acts.

Having that desire activated I remember about four months before I left Nigeria our neighbours downstairs were asked to look after me for the whole day. Whilst I was there, I remember four girls and two boys whom were brothers and sisters living there, and one of the boys I had played with before and made kites with on more than one occasion.

This particular time the boys and the two elder sisters weren't there they had left out to go shopping early in the morning with their parents so it was just me and the two girls, one was ten and the other five. We began to watch television in their front room then about two hours later the elder sister started jumping on me and play fighting with me, then we were running around their house and ended up in their bedroom.

Out of the blue we started speaking about boyfriends and girlfriends, then the elder sister of the two started saying her younger sister is my girlfriend and made us hold hands and kiss. She then suggested we take our clothes off which we did, out of respect because she was older than us, so I listened to her and then she said I should get on top of her sister which I did then we were practically carrying out a sexual act then the elder sister, took off her underwear and told me to get on top of her, which I did and we carried out a sexual act. After about twenty minutes we started to tidy the room and within ten minutes the rest of the family was back. From then on everytime I bumped into the sisters they would joke and say when am I going to marry my girlfriend, which was their five-year-old sister, and I would laugh and ask for their brother.

I remember looking at women and girls in a different light, I started to look at them with a curious mentality and imagination.

I wondered how their bodies looked, how it would feel to get on top of them it was another interest.

I would think: " I wonder if this girl or young lady wants to be my girlfriend or would like to get naked with me? I think lust kicked in there on my innocent mind.

This spirit of lust followed me from there, and later led to filthy magazines and thoughts, and a lack of respect in that area, till the age of about nineteen years old.

My first encounter and knowledge about religion was when I was aware of my grandmother praying to Allah and she would always teach me the Qur'an and tell me to always be a good boy, and to always pray five time a day! "Mind you I was at grandmother's house, at least twice a week, every week, my close aunty and cousins lived there.

My uncle and aunties also had an impact in my life, they always seemed to enjoy calling me, by my Muslim name, my grandfather named me. Which was Mohammed and seemed to enjoy emphasizing it and talking about Allah and encouraging me to pray.

I remember going to the mosque on several occasions to worship Allah having to take my slippers off and watch. I didn't really have much interest in it, it was just a going with the flow thing to me, at the time. To me, I suppose a sense of respect to my elders. I loved my grandmother very much she had bags of character, she was my mum's, mum. Sometimes when I messed around she would give me a conk on my head, which never really hurt.

The only time I remember her giving me a good hiding was when I spilled her stew. My cousin and I were play fighting, then we got very rough and knocked the big pot of stew over by mistake, we got whipped with the broom until my *"super gran"* got tired.

The only things I disliked when I went to my grandmother's place was when she would literally scrubbed our hair or should I say head with headlice soap, although my cousins or me never had any lice it was just done just in case. The other thing I disliked at my grandmother's place was the toilet, coz it 'stunk'.

That toilet was full of flies coz there was pooh all over the floor. It wasn't your average modern toilet this was a concrete open toilet with a round hole, so the only way we got rid of the waste was pouring water onto the floor, which would filter into the hole. Plus we also needed water to wash our bottoms coz there was no toilet paper, it was the local newspaper or water to wipe our behind, however we had normal toilets at my mum and dad's place.

The only time I enjoyed being a Muslim was when we celebrated Ramadan, we always had fireworks and lots of games and I would see most of my family. I enjoyed spending most of my time at my grandmother's house with about three of my cousins and my brother. It was fun with my cousins we would play fight hard, all the time and play lots of games, "you know the typical boys dangerous games. I remember playing a game, basically guessing which hand the coin was in, then to confirm my choice and swear by Allah twice that, that was my choice.

I also remember being a bit confused when I acknowledged who Jesus was, and learning about it in school. It was funny because at school I used to swear in Allah's name to prove I am telling the truth about something and other times I used to swear by Jesus because that would be another friend's religion.

One of my favourite films was actually "The Ten Commandments" a film about Moses, it's a joke coz I didn't know who the heck Moses was as I know now.

Then I was Muslim, from a Muslim background, in a Muslim family, with a Muslim name, with Muslim and Christian friends, and thought both religions were just the same thing, but different names.

"I think, I remember going to church over four times as a Muslim with my mother and father, and later realising it was just invitations my parents agreed on.

Chapter 4

Little Thief

As I've said before as a little child I never got any pocket money or sweets unless given to me by my uncle or certain old women, I think were my mother's, aunties, sisters and friends, who occasionally dropped by, who were the only people I could remember buying me stuff such as biscuits, cakes and sweets. I had goodies once in a blue moon, which was very, very 'rarely! If my mum and dad were there and I was offered money or sweets, I was taught to say: "No Thank You" which always burnt me to have to say. So this led me to my bad and "A level" habit! "Stealing"! Which stuck to me for years, my mother once said to me if I steal little things now and carry on, I would steal bigger things and would end up in jail.

I always was a good listener but terrible at learning lessons. It would go in one ear and slowly glide out the other.

I stole money to buy things. Things I longed for such as doughnuts, sweets and little toys, it might sound funny, but as a kid my frame of mind was like this. Ninety percent of the time I would get caught and get a good beating with the cane.

Let me tell you something for nothing: *"LISTEN TO YOUR PARENTS"*...

"You know something? Toys and sweets, the way it's even promoted and marketed, gets more and more advanced! You have the game boys, and roller skates, even mobile phones. Soon the kids will be driving, you never can tell what inventions and creations are coming out next.

"Only God can judge me or forgive me but I used to be a little thief!!!

As a little kid, I always used to steal money from my father's room, or car where he left loose change about.

I would take a little out of the loose coin that was there, thinking it would not be noticed or missed but I was wrong! I would always take the risk and opportunity. I think it was because I saw kids on the television treated differently and some kids around me having what I longed to have so I would try to get it myself if I could, but now realising maybe my parents couldn't afford it.

Back In South London

I came back to London on my eighth birthday, this was the real beginning of my life!

"Where should I start? My dad and I spent about two years together, that's when life went real slow, i.e. school days, week days, hours, seconds, even weekends, early years in general.

I started primary school not long after, which was a big difference to the one I attended in Nigeria, and this school was about two minutes from my house.

"I must admit I took full *"liberties".* I took the *"Mick" mate"* I stretched out all the advantages and opportunities to run wild! I inhaled "freedom.............

When I started primary school I was sharp, and on my best behaviour, that's how I was programmed at the time but when I started settling down and realizing teachers didn't beat children over here, I started picking up bad habits, which little did I know would have yet another effect on my future! I started misbehaving in class, my focus was on girls, and sweets again. I always did my homework, coz my dad did not let me watch television, and if I did, it would be for about three, four hours then I was sent to bed at *7pm.* I remember that clearly like it was last night trust!!!!

In primary school I found it fun, it's like I just 'kicked back' and broke loose, I used to look out, for some of the little kids, especially the ones that just came out of infant's school.

I always made sure they would report to me, if anyone wanted to bully them and a few times they did report to me. I fly kicked the person that bullied them, that's how I used hurt people back then. I also had a black Jamaican friend called Hainsley Dickson. He was my first best friend and we were a bad influence on each other.

He was also like a bodyguard to me because he was one of the strongest in our primary school everyone was afraid of him. We used to pretend we were the "T birds" out of the film GREASE, and we used to make three specific girls the pink ladies, which we idolised so much. Back then that's how far we took it, we went all out straight up and down.

Hainsley always said he would get his aunty to get us both leather jackets with "T Birds" on it. We did front flips together and also used to show off our dancing skills together, we stole chocolate biscuits out of the reward tin together, and played mummy and daddies with girls together.

Hainsley and me just clicked, those that can relate, you know, that was the in game to get to kiss the girls *"back in the days"* in primary school.

London, London, London. I loved London.

At primary school I really, really enjoyed swimming, although I couldn't, I was fascinated with the girls as they swam in their swimming gear. I am proud of myself for completing my *100 meters*, I still have my badge for that hanging around in my box of memories. I also enjoyed playing rounders, which was a game similar to baseball, or cricket, with a bat, I loved acting, doing pantomimes, and the bonuses which were quizzes, and listening to stories.

There was so much things Hainsley and I did together most of it was based around school, coz for one, my dad never ever let me play out.

One week, out of the blue, my dad gave me the dinner money for the week to give to the secretary.

I guess he was very busy that Monday, coz he normally would take me to school every Monday, and go into the office to give the secretary my school dinner money for the week, but not this occasion.

Instead of me giving that money to the secretary I kept it in my pocket and told Hainsley, we are going to sneak out of school at lunch time and we are gonna have McDonald's. He enthusiastically agreed.

Anyways, that lunch time we both did manage to sneak out, and ran all the way to McDonalds and I spent the money on two McDonalds meals for both of us, which was at the time, *"quality"*.

After that we ran back to school, and we sneaked in just in time for class.

Now when Tuesday came I couldn't eat coz the headmaster had to check who's parents had paid for lunch that week. He probably presumed I had packed lunch for the week, so what I had to do was sneak out of school, every day that week. I would go home and get in by climbing in the house through the window, which was dangerous because it was a second floor flat and I had to climb up the pipe to get into the top tiny window, which was awkward to get into, if I had ever slipped wrong I could have fell head first either on the balcony or over the balcony. Coz we lived in flats on second floor.

Anyways I would manage to climb in, then make myself a sandwich quickly, then quickly rush back to school. Thursday came and it was impossible to sneak out, so that day I told my teacher I was hungry and I didn't have any packed lunch, so she took me to the canteen and cooked me food.

Little did I know she was so worried about me that she told the headmaster who told my dad.

On Friday I was in class. I remember my dad coming into the classroom looking at me with anger, for about three seconds probably thinking what on earth did I do with the money then he left.

On my way home, that day after school I asked six people to follow me home including Hainsley.

I told everyone I was going to get beats with the belt, well more than six people followed me home. I got to the door knocked on it whilst my friends from school stood behind me, then my dad opened the door. I went straight into the living room, I took a deep breath then I said: "good afternoon". He laid there with the newspaper over his face, then looked at me with a vex look, once then continued to read his paper, I thought I had got off the hook, I went to the door and whispered to my friends through the letter box to wait, then I sat in my room for a while then, I thought okay my dad's fine, so I went into the living room to say good afternoon again. My dad ignored me and he headed towards the door locked all three locks, that's when I knew what was gonna happen, he got the belt and beat the truth out of me. God it was painful it's hard being a man sometimes!

My dad never gave me the money again, if he had I would have gladly made sure the secretary got it straight away this time. "Talking about the secretary" I remember when she left the office door open one morning, I knew all the children's dinner money was in the office, because I didn't get pocket money and I craved for certain things, I went into that office and stole all the money by emptying all the coins into my socks.

I wonder what happened to her, boy she must have thought she was going nuts!

Burning My House

I was a very independent young man at the age of eight, I was always left in the house by myself it was only my dad and myself at the time in London. He had to go to work every day in the day, so when I had holidays I never saw him until the evening I remember having to record "Top Of The Pops" for him, a music show in the weekday.

Sometimes I used to be scared and lonely and couldn't wait till he got back.I didn't want to see a ghost again.

One particular week during the Christmas period, my dad was off work that day so he went Christmas shopping, my dad said I should turn the heater down when the living room is very hot. It was one of those wall electric gas heaters, which sometimes you used a match to light.

That day I was watching one of my favourite adventure television series "NIGHT RIDER" it was after one of my other favourites "THE A TEAM". I started playing Lego at the same time, I always enjoyed playing with toys especially Lego figures, I had a huge collection too. How? "You guessed it. I stole them all from primary school. Well as I was watching "NIGHT RIDER" and playing with Lego, I started concentrating more on my toys, coz I had seen this particular episode of "NIGHT RIDER" so I played with my toys and took one Lego figure, just playing imagining and pretending, one of my Lego men threw the other in a fire.

What I actually did was put my Lego into the heater and to my shock the Lego caught on fire straight away, lit up quick and was burning and melting away. It started burning my fingers so I panicked and threw the burning Lego into the bin, which had a carrier bag wrapped around it, and which I now know, is highly flammable. It lit up catching on fire, there was a table there that had a tablecloth on it, which hanged near the bin the fire caught onto that and started spreading.

I was in shock, I felt stuck there out of shock. I stood still for about a minute or two watching the fire spread, and getting bigger. I didn't know what the heck to do? I was just standing there baffled witnessing, what I had done, and thinking about what my dad was going to do.

This all happened so fast and in a matter of seconds the living room was on fire and instantly filled with smoke, suddenly I started coughing, that's when I came to my senses and realised the house was really burning to the ground. I ran towards the front door (this was the second time in my childhood I nearly died).

I finally made it to the front door contemplating whether I should use the kitchen window or not because the door might be locked fortunately it wasn't. I was too short and the little handle was a bit high so I started chocking, coughing and cried some more as the smoke was filling out into the passage. Finally God's grace kicked in, I couldn't see the handle anymore so I started panicking, and started crying, then I started saying Jesus, Allah, God help me.

Seconds later I found the handle and opened the door, the smoke rushed out with me then I remembered my dad normally locks the door if he leaves me in the house, but thank God he didn't this time. In the day time or if my dad was just going out for a few hours he wouldn't lock the door so the rule was, not to answer the door to anyone.

Anyways as I said I got the door open somehow, how? I don't know but I do know now God was there.

As soon as the door swung open the smoke came rushing out and I started screaming help, coz that's what I saw people do in films, when they are in trouble.

Now this is how I know God almighty works, God almighty sends the people you would never thought would have help, to help you.

A white kid called Kirk with freckles, who I didn't get on with at school who used to try and spit on me sometimes, saw little me from his first floor block of flats opposite and heard me crying, screaming, shouting and waving my hands. He smiled because he must have thought I was playing until he noticed the smoke oozing out of my flat and ran and called his mother then pointed at me and she called the fire brigade.

"I HAD BURNT MY DAD'S HOUSE DOWN".

When he came I was glad to see him, and that was the first time he gave me a hug and didn't shout or beat me. I was shocked too, he thought I was in the fire. We spent that Christmas in a bed and breakfast hostel.

Mrs Cummings

The social services people threatened to take me into care after that fire incident, if my dad never found me a nanny or baby sitter.

I was nine, and it was against the law to leave me at home at that age.

So my dad found a short-term solution, which was letting his friend baby sit me.

A lady called aunty Kinta offered to, I was looking forward to it. She had two sons called Victor and David.

Because David was the eldest one he looked after us while their mum (aunty Kinta) went to work for 6 hours. My first time at aunty Kinta's I just did my homework, ate and went to bed.

But as time went on I began to be playful. This is where things started going pear shaped. I started to hate going to her house coz Victor cooked me food I did not like sometimes and forced me to eat it. Then abuse started.

Victor and David would abuse me by wrestling with me, punching me, kicking me and pulling down my trousers and clothes.

Victor was 14 and his brother was 9 they were both bigger and stronger than me. I was only little at the time so they would beat me up using the television (WWF) wrestling moves on me. It hurt man, and it always use to make me cry, coz I could never beat them, coz they were far stronger than I was.

I remember a dreadful time when they pretended I was a girl and started trying to penetrate me by trying to put their penis into my bottom but I wouldn't hold still so they would hold me down and rub themselves on me, like I was a girl. I really disliked it and I didn't ever look forward to going there anymore!

After a while of going to aunty Kinta's house I really started to get fed up of the abuse, so I decided I would fight back.

My first attempt, Victor got his little brother David to beat me up, second attempt Victor and his brother David beat me up.

There were no more attempts after that. I had come to a conclusion that they were just too strong for me to handle so I took the last option, which was telling their mum. Who gave them both a few slaps, back hands and a haaaaaaaaard belt beating.

The advantage of that at the time was that I saw them both cry like little babies. They got a good old fashion thrashing from their mum that seemed like revenge and justice for me. But when I went round after that they had plans for me!

Victor prepared a meal for all three of us.

The usual french fries, sausages and potatoe waffles. It appeared that Victor and David were being nice to me for once, I was like maybe that thrashing aunty Kinta delivered to them paid off.

Well so I thought. I started to head for the kitchen with my belly feeling nice and chest pushed out feeling macho, looking forward to a nice cold glass of tap water, suddenly David grabs me from behind then Victor comes from nowhere with a white Tesco supermarket carrier bag in his hand. I was confused? David is still holding me from behind with a tight grip laughing his head off suddenly Victor proceeds to put the carrier bag over my head then he tightens it and ties it to my neck.

At this point I was frozen and in deep fear 'fearing the worst'. The carrier bag was over my head and I started to suffocate.

After about five seconds I ran out of breath so I used all the strength in me to punch and kick coz I did not want to die, coz I felt like I was dying.

As I was punching and kicking at the shadows David was caught with one somewhere on his head and fell to the floor! At this stage Victor was pushing and spinning me around in the living room. I was panicking trying to loosen or rip the carrier bag off my head so I could breathe.

I suddenly dropped on the floor weak with my last breath, struggling, shaking and suffocating, just at the brink of blacking out and dying. Victor pokes his finger through the carrier bag and started to laugh hysterically with his brother David. I got some air and started to breathe with relief, I started to cough and cry with half of the carrier bag ripped, hanging around my neck.

Victor and David carried on laughing then started to tease me and call me a cry baby. *"Cry baby"*, *"cry baby"*, *"come here cry baby,"* they continued to call me and laugh.

At this point I was so scared but also angry coz they could have killed me, so in frustration I put my fists up and screamed: *"come on then"*, *"come on then"*. I got beaten up of course and started to feel sorry for myself.

Later that day late in the evening aunty Kinta had not got back from work yet, this seemed later than usual, it was 9pm so we had to get to bed before she showed up so I went into the bathroom for a quick bath. I proceeded to take my bath.

Victor and David burst into the bathroom then out of nowhere they start to laugh looking at me in the bath tub, they gazed at each other then Victor pulls out his penis and started to urinate on me. Then David started to do the same, both laughing thinking it was hysterical. I try to shield myself by putting my arms in front of my face but the urine started to get in my eyes and mouth.

They both urinated all over my face, my hair, my back and body, I just kneeled there helpless and started to cry crazily. I didn't move until I stopped crying.

I had cried until my eyes were red and hurting. My head started to hurt and I felt weak so I stopped feeling sorry for myself and grabbed some antiseptic (Dettol) and poured it into a bucket and started to wash my skin, suddenly Victor and David burst into the bathroom again holding their penis up in their hand and started spraying me again with urine laughing their heads off then running back out. I had no energy to cry anymore so I just took it and attempted to take a bath again.

The last time I went to aunty Kinta's place I went to a white garment church called BROTHER HOOD FELLOWSHIP. They told me that I had to take off my shoes when I stepped into their place of worship and told me that I had to get my father to get me a white robe to wear next time I come to their church, because it is their religion to serve Jesus Christ by wearing white robes before coming into the church?

That was the last straw for me. I hated the white garment church, I hated Victor and David and I hated going to aunty Kinta's house, so I kept begging my dad not to make me go to aunty Kinta's place, and told my dad I was being bullied and beaten up every time by her kids.

So I eventually got my wish and I did not have to see aunty Kinta's face, 5th floor two bed flat, Victor and David again!

My dad managed to find me a nanny that was when I moved to "Surrey" a place outside London.

I was looked after by a lovely old white lady called Eileen Cummings, I called her Mrs Cummings, she was married and lived in a three bedroom terraced house with a hard working Irish husband, who was a builder, and a black foster lady in her twenties called Sharon.

She owned two German shepherd dogs and a cat. I lived there full-time and went to primary school there.

Besides a mixed race boy, I "seriously" was the only black kid, in the school! So you could imagine everyone was fascinated, and I had a lot of attention, I was a little loud mouth, loved girls and was obsessed with Michael Jackson.

I could do most of his dance moves, which boys and girls always begged me to do.

I remember the first week I started, I spoke to a pretty brunette white girl called Toni and told her I liked her and asked her to be my girlfriend, she agreed. You know when you are kids it's okay, it's almost like a game, shortly after little did I know Toni told everyone she was going out with me which meant she was my girlfriend. On that Friday a lot of little boys were coming up to me asking me if it was true, because she was one of the prettiest girls in the school.

A lot of kids asked if I was going out with her, but I didn't have a clue what they really meant, so I was smiling and said no, because I thought it meant I was going out somewhere with her.

Anyways the news got back to her and she was heart broken coz she thought I meant we were not boyfriend and girlfriend, obviously a big misunderstanding.

I told her I was sorry and we were boyfriend and girlfriend again. I actually went to her house that Saturday. Her parent's house was heavy, it was "Tha Boom", I met her mum. Toni introduced me to her as her boyfriend.

I was so shy, she thought I was just Toni's cute little black boyfriend, but as in boy and friend. She left us both alone outside the door with drinks and biscuits, as I couldn't go into her house because she was told, no one was allowed. I did use her toilet and I remember locking myself in there for about *20* minutes just staring and lying on the floor talking to Toni from the toilet, it was a big toilet bigger than my current bedroom at home, believe me it was big. I also cracked jokes, pretending I was farting in her toilet, it was fun, we hugged and held hands, that's all we ever did, for about two weeks, then we broke up.

We never even kissed once, two weeks later I started to go out with a white girl called Vicky, the first girl in my life, which I really loved, "hey I was nine and thought I was in love? I engraved her name in the sand and played kiss chase with her.

I also remember spending an entire weekend with her, we chilled out in the woods where we nearly got naked, but we always got caught before I rubbed off my bad influence on her. We walked in the park, hand in hand kissing all day and everyday we got together. We would even hide out in school to kiss. "Not French kissing, or tongues, didn't know about that then, okay, "I thought I'd say that just to make things clear for the record!

One Monday she came to school and I smiled and winked at her, but she didn't wink back, I knew something was up she walked up to me slowly head down and said that she can't be my girlfriend anymore, because her dad said she don't want her to go out with black boys. My heart was so broken I remember crying just before going into class, a nine year old in love, I was in love, I really thought I was!

That break time I saw a boy cuddling her and smiling, so I made a run up and fly kicked him in his back, "boy it hurt him and he cried, lucky my teachers didn't tell Mrs Cummins coz my dad would also hear about it. Three weeks later I went out with a girl called Kelly, which was funny coz she had a Portuguese boy friend called Gavin who found out and didn't like black people so he beat me up!

School in Surrey was good, I had so much freedom it was so different from Nigeria I even forgot about Nigeria, and did what I felt like. My tutor was great she was a good teacher. Her name was Mrs Metcalf, I think she was from Australia! Now knowing about accents she definitely was Australian.

The first day I went swimming, everyone swam all the way to the deep end, so for some strange reason, I tried it too? When I got half way I couldn't go anymore I slowly started sinking and drowning, I couldn't even shout for help I was drowning and on my last breath the instructor managed to pull me up on a third attempt with some rod thing, I was so close to totally drowning, I wonder now why she didn't just dive in and get me, *God is good!*

Later I that week I met my best friend in primary school. A white boy called Scott Chambers. Mrs Cummins, coincidently use to baby sit him when he was little.

We went everywhere together to primary school, tree climbing in the woods, youth clubs, parks, the circus, playing out also bike riding. I nearly forgot I stole a bicycle in order for me to do that'.

I was at the park one day playing football with Scott and another team, then from nowhere one of the boys playing against us started to call me names? That same boy started having a tantrum and complaining his bicycle chain was loose, the tire was flat and his bicycle was crap. He screamed that he was going to leave it and his dad would buy him a new one. So he left it.

It was one of those bicycles called 'Chopper' with long handle bars and a small leaver for the 3 gears in the middle of the bike frame, to cut the long story short I took it! I loved that bicycle it looked like a Harley Davison motorbike.

Scott and I went bike riding one day and I was going to dare to do a stunt with my Chopper. I wanted to show off because there were three boys around so I rode the bike off something high and thought I was going to land whilst lifting the handle bars like the kids on the stunt bike programme called 'Kick Start' on TV in those times, but it didn't work like that, and I ended up falling flat on my face cracking my front tooth.

It was the first time going to the dentist and I was so scared when the dentist fixed my tooth, all my teeth kind of just went yellow for some reason after that. That was one of the reasons I got gold put on my front teeth after I turned eighteen.

In Surrey when I had my bicycle, I always used to ride a little far out to a shop called SPAR to buy my favourite lolly pop sweets and steal a pack of chocolate biscuits or kinder egg chocolates, mainly kinder egg chocolates, it was a chocolate that is in a shape of a small egg, that has a miniature toy inside. I never had enough money, I only had *10 or 20p* so I stole it one day I nearly got caught.

I had a lot of fun on that bike of mine after Mrs Cummings's husband fixed it for me. I went to the shop with it and to play out with, I could go long distances with my bicycle, which was so adventurous.

Mrs Cummings was a nice nanny she had a big family we often went to her children's houses they had nice houses, she bought me Easter eggs at Easter and she always let me play out with my friends she gave me *10p* a day after buying the paper, she took me food shopping with her and let me pick some of the things I liked to eat, I thought I was in heaven then.

I now know there ain't such things as fairies but when, one of my tooth fell out one week she told me to put my tooth under my pillow and the fairy God mother would take it and leave some money. When I did it the next morning I looked under my pillow and to my surprise found money and no tooth I was excited and amazed from that day onwards I believed in Fairy God mothers, and Father Christmas for a long time.

The only thing I didn't like for the few months I lived with her, although I managed to eat dinner all the time, I was always uncomfortable and put off coz the dog always ate off the same plates everyone used. Which put me off eating many times, I was also put off, what she cooked, and missed my mum's cooking. I was scared of the dogs and hated them and their stench, "they stunk man" I was also put off when she used to lick and spit on her hanky to use to wipe my face, when it was dirty, and the cat scratched me once, so I never liked it. I have never liked pets anyway, or anything fury, they put me off especially their smell.

I always did what I was told when I was in Surrey, coz Mrs Cummings spoke to my dad over the phone everytime, she needed to find out stuff, and I knew she would tell my dad if I started acting up.

One day I did act up! Everytime I used to go to the shop to buy the paper for Mrs Cummings on certain occasions she would tell me to take *10* or *20p* for myself in her bag where she kept her purse. Sometimes I took about two pounds other times I would take just a bit more than I was supposed to.

One morning I went in her bag and unzipped the wrong bit, and I noticed wads of money (fresh bank notes).

I took no notice of it for about two weeks, then one week Scott wasn't around and I was with the other boys around the area I lived in, and all of us took a trip to the local newsagents shop that sold everything. It also happened to be where I bought tined cat and dog food for the pets, and I was well known by the shop keeper there called Raj, so I never stole from his shop because most of the groceries were bought from his shop by Mrs Cummings and I was with her the majority of the time. So I had a respect for his shop to a certain extent!

While I was in the shop with the boys, I started imagining what it would be like to buy everyone anything in the shop. I told everyone I was going to buy everyone anything they wanted in the shop next week, all the kids were laughing then we went home.

The next morning I just thought I would check to see if the wads of money was there, to my surprise it was so without thinking I took £10 to school and hid it in my sock, after school I rode my bike to my favourite super market Spar, and this time paid for my chocolate kinder eggs. When I got to my area all the boys were coincidently there.

So I said: "who wants anything from the shop", anything at all, everyone said yes, but thought I was joking but all headed for the shop with me. I then bought everyone anything they wanted.

I had started a habit of stealing money from Mrs Cummings's bag without her knowing. I repeated this the next week, and then the next week, I took more this time. I took £20 I spent some of it at school, and at my favourite shop Spar, I bumped into the boys from my area again.

This time I had much more money so I decided to change the whole £15 note into £1 coins and scrambled it, I shouted: *"SCRAMBLE"* and threw all the pound coins in the air, after I did that everyone started talking about what I did and I had become popular overnight people would come knocking at my door asking for me, my school started getting suspicious and I over heard Mrs Cummings telling her husband she thinks she might have lost some money about £40 somehow, that was the fifth week I must have taken money, it totalled to about £90 I had stolen if not more.

The following morning I had no idea, Mrs Cummings had counted the money so I took £10 thinking she would not notice but that day she was called to my school, because I had been misbehaving at school and rumours had been going around that I had given a lot of money away which was making me popular.

That day everything seemed to happen so fast, Mrs Cummings confronted me and asked me if I took £10, that morning, I just froze then she asked me again, I froze even more in a daze, baffled as to what I should do or say. She then told me to empty out my pockets, when I had finished £9 was found, all was exposed and everything linked together and made sense to Mrs Cummings, "I must admit I felt very guilty and she didn't deserve that", she was so kind to me.

My mum had only been in London a few weeks, and I remember speaking to her about a week ago telling her I was doing good, but I was also missing her and home. So I felt very stupid.

That evening Mrs Cummings phoned my dad and told him the whole story, I sat on the stairs listening to all she said and felt so ashamed.

I was so scared about what was going to happen, what kind of beats I was going to get, and all the rest of it.

Mr and Mrs Cummings drove me home that night in shock and in a sense of betrayal. When I got back home in London my heart was beating very fast, I felt shameful, hot and cold and like a big let down to my parents. They were so embarrassed.

I had to admit it, but I still lied as to how much money I stole, I said I took about *£40* another lie, *£40* was alot to my dad at that time plus my mum had just arrived in London.

Imagine if I had said I took about *£90* I wonder if I still would be living? Coz boy come to think of it, that was a whole heap of cash.

Back In South London Again

Aged ten, I was back in London, with my mum and dad, this time they were more strict with me, coz they had plans for my brother and I to stay in Surrey with Mrs Cummings, when he arrived in London. I messed that up and as far as my parents were concerned I wasn't to be trusted!

I was back at the original school I started, so I just got on with it. At this time my maths was really slacking and my English was changing, and I desired to play out all the time, which I wasn't allowed to do! Again.

This stage I did not pay much attention to my studies I was more interested in girls, chocolates and porn magazines I stole from the shop. I got caught one day with that filth in my room, same procedure as before my mum gave me a good hot slap.

Summer was a very good excuse to go out, I was always afraid to ask my dad coz he would shout at me like I just stole something, so I used to kind of play it by asking my mum to tell my dad. Which worked, coz I washed the plates, swept the floor and done any homework so the only agenda I had was to be ready so I could play out.

Well did it did happen? Yes it did at last.

I had one hour every time, I always just about got a squeeze..........

The only problem was, I always got home late, coz I was always exploring when playing out. I would go to friends houses, empty flats, the tunnels, the favourite place was a place called "the adventure" a park which was built like an adventure with lots of wood, plat forms, tree houses and long ropes to swing and climb from.

The place was addictive, and fun I met so much people there including girls although this place was five minutes away from home I still got home late it was that much fun!

I always got grounded, but again I always sneaked out and majority of the time had girls and boys over the house when my parents were out.

Again in London my parents worked very hard. My mum was a chef and my dad was a taxi driver, they both worked hard. I hardly saw them during the week.

I would feel so lonely and bored and sometimes scared especially when lights went out because the electric ran out. I used to watch many horror films especially Dracula, and I believed in ghosts coz I remember seeing one and I know, what I saw in the past, so I would rush around sometimes like a headless chicken paranoid and would hide or find my bed sheet and put it over my whole body hiding. I started sneaking over to the community youth centre near the adventure playground. When my parents were at work. I enjoyed table tennis, which I was just a natural at, darts and all that jazz. Lots of kids smoked in there, I was always fascinated watching kids being able to do what they wanted, without any of the adults in the centre telling the kids what to do, or not to smoke, or not to swear. The only thing that wasn't allowed was fighting. That was paradise again to me, I remember when I properly joined the centre and the adult youth worker told me the rules were: no stealing, fighting, drugs or weapons allowed, anything else was fine then I was given free condoms. I had never seen what that was, so I opened it when I got home and found out later what they were for.

Everytime I snuck out I had to climb back in by the window because I didn't have my own set of keys.

At the youth centre I started meeting new friends and started mixing in with certain groups and was so fascinated how the boys and girls blew rings of smoke out their mouths.

I wanted to know how to do it too so I tried to see if I could steal a pack of cigarettes from the shops, but that was impossible so I watched the other kids as they asked each other for cigarettes. I asked and to my shock I got a cigarette, "my first cigarette" when I tried to light it, it took ages and when I finally did get it lit, every drag I inhaled I coughed like I never coughed before, which put me off it straight away. The kids I hanged around with smoked, so I felt I had to get with the programme, so I always forced myself to smoke, just to fit in, so I basically wouldn't get bullied or teased.

My parents were unaware of this, but one particular morning before I went to primary school, I went to buy the newspaper for my dad, as I did every morning seven days a week. On my way to the shop I saw a half smoked lit cigarette on the floor so I picked it up and wiped off the lipstick that was on it, presumably a woman had been smoking it.

Then I put that dirty cigarette in my mouth and started smoking it, after smoking it for some reason I enjoyed it, I felt I was getting better, I didn't cough I just spat on the floor, and I kind of felt like a man.

I was the man! When I got home, as I passed the newspaper to my dad, my mum smelled my hand, and immediately took the paper from my dad and smelled the newspaper and told my dad the paper smelt of cigarette.

My dad wasn't bothered but my mum sure was, so she immediately told me to let her smell my breath, I froze trying to avoid the possible question and shook my head saying I wasn't smoking then she got up grabbed me by my shirt collar, and pulled me towards her face. We were face to face and she told me again: *"let me smell your breath"*. When I breathed out my mum turned her face in disgust and literally punched me in my mouth, and shouted at me. That was the first and last time my dad sided with me and shouted at my mum for doing that.

I don't think she realised how hard she had hit me, but one of my front bottom teeth caved in and started bleeding and I ran into the bathroom, crying with pain, agony and shock. *That taught me a lesson for a long time.*

Chapter 5

Knowledge Wisdom Faith

Watch catch and digest this revelation! When you get the *'knowledge'* you get the information the *'know how'*, you get to know about something! Then comes the *'understanding'* you know what's popping, you're clear on stuff and have a revelation things are exposed to you then you get the *'wisdom'* you know, right and wrong, good and bad you become wise!

God created us all so we all have a common kind of wisdom, but the true wisdom is when you activate God in you. How do you do that? By acknowledging God! *Now that's wisdom!* Check out these scriptures in the Bible (God's Mind) **Proverbs Chapter 1 2 3 4 5 6 7 and 8** it clarifies knowledge, wisdom and understanding and you realise to be wise is to fear God!

So many people have gone astray in this world, there are loads of these people I have met and have said all religions and Gods are the same.

"NO", no, no, no, no, no. All religions are not the same, people study religions and think *'yep'* they are scholars, and do not have a solid belief! But deep down they are still baffled? They create their own God, but this is where one has flopped.

The more you keep studying different religions you will get confused?

There is one truth and one truth only! *"You better recognise!*

The Holy Bible (God's Mind) for instance is clear and straightforward, but people make it so complicated. We want instant questions answered!

Without getting to know the Word (The Bible).

A friend once said the bible is **Basic**, Instruction, **Before**, You Leave, **Earth!**

I would say that's a good definition! Everything is in the Bible (God's Mind) Science, psychology, history, geography, the beginning and the end.

I'll tell you something about my experience with the Bible (God's Mind) and with a lot of other true Christian people such as pastors, bishops, reverends, fathers, priests and all these titles of Christian leaders.

For every meaning, every word in the Bible (God's Mind) it unfolds and reveals itself in confirmation to you. It always guides you and confirms when you're doing the right things or when you're doing the wrong things. God uses 'people' to confirm His Word and deliver His Word.

The Word of God is Holy, moral and powerful and it's God, who is love!

As an individual, you need to keep pressing into the Bible (God's Mind) coz it has a lot of parables and sometimes one tries to figure out too much in one go?

You need to get a foundation of a right and real understanding, something that is not weird, something solid. Which is God Elohim that means strong one in Hebrew, God Jehovah. Don't get mixed up now, about that name Jehovah cause I'm not talking about anything to do with Jehovah's Witness. Jehovah just simply means God too.

"One needs knowledge, wisdom and faith in this mashed up corrupt world we live in.

Some people believe in the devil, a lucky charm, money, the brick wall, cars, the government, weed, marijuana, human beings, mum, dad, or something. That something that you just can't put a finger on. There is something far beyond these things, all you gots to do is press into the spiritual realm to find out the right and willing way of what the Holy Bible (God's Mind) says to you.

You need to believe in a God, meaning you need to know God's character not just a God, the right God, the God that loves and forgives and will give you spiritual gifts, authority and power! The God I personally know and the God you can build a relationship with. The God that has character, the God who is awesome, the God that keeps it real, the God who is merciful, kind, inspirational, full of integrity, full of love, kindness, forgiveness, consideration and class.

Let me show you how you know you're on the right track with a spot on belief.

Number one, when you start desiring to pray for people other than yourself! **Two**, when you start feeling compassionate and repenting daily coz you hate sin. **Three**, being grateful and fighting to live right, as you adopt this mentality, you will find that's when some of the mysteries of God start being revealed to you, especially about the Bible (God's Mind) and knowledge, wisdom and understanding become more clear coz God hides nothing!

In the Bible (God's Mind) in **1 Corinthians Chapter 2 Verse 9** it says that the "Eye has not seen or ear heard what God has prepared for those that love Him". *Wow that is deep.*

When God said: *"Ask it shall be given"* He ain't joking about, you know. He has actually has given, He ain't gonna give to you again, cause He can't. He has already said it is given so it is given? What is given? Whatever desires you are asking for.

"That is desires that are righteous and beneficial that is, such as

"GOD'S PROMISES", don't get it twisted.

So when you keep asking, you keep repeating yourself, you have no knowledge or understanding it is there, I must admit I forget sometimes, but I realise quick and then think what am I doing? The Holy Spirit prompts me, then I change my words and just say thank you to God and hold on to the belief. That's knowledge, wisdom and faith again they all work hand in hand.

So the next time when you knock, know that the door is open alls you gots to do is walk through it, walk in your blessing, when you ask, know that you have received it! Believe and stand on it coz it's God's Word and God does not lie, it ain't my words! Know that when you seek, you have really found what you are looking for! Coz it's there, made available from God, so enjoy the benefits of it and take the next step of acting. *ACTION!* *"It's all faith*

"One Sunday the year of 2001 I went to see my friend that I hadn't seen in ages, after church so I bought some chocolates, coz I dislike going to friends or families houses empty handed, plus it was Christmas.

I remember back in the days I would bring a bottle of wine, a bag of weed, or some potent ganja, skunkweed as it were, to this particular friend's house for her mum and both of us to *"blaze", "burn it down haaaaaaaaaard"* (smoke).

This particular day my friend was not there but her mum was, so I started speaking with her mum. Her mum is a white woman who I felt was sincerely real, outgoing, full of character. She was funny, clued up and could relate to me. Maybe coz her baby father was black.

I always had an interesting conversation with her mum when she was not around, which always went on for hours. Trust me her mum could talk! I remember one occasion in my teenage years when I hot wired a car and stole it, coz the widows was left open. It was such a buzz at the time to steal that car, it was the first one I stole and drove by myself, that day I drove it to her house and her mother asked me where I stole it from and I told her.

Her mother had such a great sense of humour, she didn't condone the wrong things I did or all of my actions, but she understood, and accepted me for who I was at the time, which was a teenager and a criminal. I realise now that she used a lot of reverse psychology when she spoke to me in those days, I supposed she always did that to find out what I had been up to or done so she could give me advice and more importantly understand me.

Her mum would advise me and constantly tell me to stay out of trouble, coz if I didn't I would end up in jail. She always used to share a lot of jokes and funny situations with me.

Anyways this particular Sunday in 2001, after she hugged me and said: *"thanks"*, for the box of chocolates she then put a spliff in her mouth and started smoking it and said: *"You look smart"*, then she said: *"but then again you've always dressed smart"*, then she added: *"what have you been up to these days"*? *"Are you keeping out of trouble Teslim?* I humbly said: *"yes"* and told her: *"I had been on this God thing and church! For the past ten months, I have been serious with God and church that's what I've been up to"*. I could tell she noticed something different about me, she could tell I had gone through a drastic change, that I was not that same teenager that was a criminal or that was driving that stolen car!

So she sarcastically said: *"So are you a believer a born-again?* I said: *"yes"* confidently, and replied: *"I'm born again, reborn, brand new, living right!* She then said she used to go to church when she was young, in Wales and then flipped the script and said: *"God is within you, Jesus isn't real"*, and said that she was happy I found God instead of something else. And then kind of contradicted herself saying: *"And at least 'God'* then added: *'Jesus' gives you hope init Teslim?*

In my mind I agreed with the Jesus gives you hope part, but I disagreed with the Jesus isn't real part, and said to her: *"Jesus is real"*. And asked her why she felt Jesus isn't real? She replied saying: *"People created Jesus, the Bible, and God as a figure, so people would live right! But it's good that you feel good, that's what it does, it makes you feel good, but there really is no Jesus; there is some kind of God.* Then she added: *"No one knows how we humans were created"*.

Wow looking back on this, she was saying some key things such as Jesus makes you feel good, and the living right part, but had lost faith to enjoy those benefits.

She then proceeded to talk about her priest in Wales where she used to live with her parents as a teenager, whom was caught out and left her town because he committed adultery and slept with a variety of women in the congregation.

The town he lived in also found out he had human testicles, penises, and fingers and all sorts in jars that he stored in his basement where he lived.

The town also discovered he took all these human parts from dead bodies that were buried from some of the church members families in the congregation, he buried and conducted funerals for.

"I thought that was shabby!

She then started saying: *"What kind of man is that, he was so quick to judge people and tell people what to do and how to conduct themselves and he turns out to be a "perv" a nasty pervert.*

So I said: *"Don't you believe in heaven and hell?* She said: *"No",* bluntly, so I just instantly replied back saying: *"Well I believe in Jesus".* *Heaven and hell is real and I am going to heaven.* I told her I would bring her to church and added: *"Jesus loves you".*

After I said that, as she was pouring herself a glass of wine, I then started thinking about everything she said. It had me thinking.

My focus was a bit dazed, but then my knowledge, understanding and wisdom kicked back in. I was focused again and my spirit started to remind me I know my God, I have a relationship with Him, He has given me peace. Further more I can't even listen to this woman, I can't take her advice anymore. I have the wisdom of God now, and she is confused at the moment, I can see she is disappointed in church, and her former priest, but that just goes to show *'no one'* is perfect and people make mistakes, everyone makes mistakes, but it should not stop us from losing faith. In her case, she had lost faith, and I needed to pray for her.

Plus everything she was saying to me, was her belief and opinion under the influence of drugs and being high from smoking weed. So she was talking to me with a drugged up *'state of mind',* which was in her hand, and it had intoxicated her mind so I couldn't listen to her and agree with what she was saying.

"Damn she was high on drugs". Like I used to be high with her!!!

'Man' drugs does really make you talk some rubbish! *Trust.*

"I still have nuff respect for her though and still love her for who she is, but I cannot take her advice!

I remember when I used to *"blaze"* (smoke) with her but those days are now gone! Furthermore in our conversation she said she was going to church on Christmas day straight after the pub or bar so she must know deep down Jesus is real. It's the devil in play again, messing with her mind and trying to blind her eyes. In a way though, I could see that she did not want to admit or feel guilty, she was running and hiding from the truth. Which is Jesus.

In a way I also don't blame her one hundred percent coz, she had been through a lot.

I am not saying Christians are perfect coz there are a lot of sincere people in the world who are non Christians that also try to make a difference, help the poor and all that jazz let me tell you something for nothing, if individuals, are good or nearly perfect unless they believe in Jesus and the Bible (God's Mind) and they grab that foundation of wisdom they are not sniffing heaven, and they will definitely not have full focus, and peace!

Chapter 6

Peace Power Perception

Some people say: *"oh Christians are some weak sad people who hope all the time"*. Another common one, people or so called atheist use.

"Oh just another religion or religious group who need something to believe in or run back to for help".

As a matter of fact every one needs something to have faith in or run back to!

Check this out in the Bible (God's Mind) In **John Chapter 3 verse 16 Jeremiah Chapter 29 verse 11 to 13.**

So for God sakes run to the right person, press into God Jehovah Jireh our provider, Yahweh GOD.

People who say Christians (Christ like people) are weak are in fact jokers, coz the truth is the people who say that, are in fact lost themselves or should I say ignorant.

You might try to reverse it and say: *"oh yeah Christians are ignorant"*, in some cases you may meet an ignorant Christian that just rams Jesus down your throat and tells you what to do and does not want to listen to what you've got to say, and may come at you with condemnation or even judge you.

But what we true Christians (Christ like people) are trying to do is help you by exposing the truth and show you things that will change your life and direct you so you will have peace!!!!!!!!!!!!

Real Christians aren't some frail, flimsy, flaky, people.

Becoming a Christian ain't easy, you inherit *'responsibility'* no one said it would be easy, but that eternal peace and power you activated, cannot be accessed anywhere else.

When you become a Christian you have to constantly battle against evil to put good and righteousness into action.

A Christian is a strong person who is eager to secure their future and eternal life when they die. By becoming a Christian you have activated the God in you, the devil keeps trying to tempt you and fight the God activated in you, out of you. That's why we battle every day, but the fact is, the battle is already won! By Jesus, we have just got to fight it until He comes back! Fight the temptations, immoral sex, drugs, getting drunk, money, fame, fantasy, and vanity.

"Guess what though? That battle gets easier, when you identify with more of that power you have activated, who is God, so circumstances and temptations are just "MINOR". It gets to a point where you don't even react coz whatever comes your way is no longer a challenge it's expected! "Wow I'm encouraging myself. Situations and temptations can't even sway you no more coz you relate to peace. What's that peace? That peace is "God", "Love," Heaven" and "Jesus"

The relationship with peace starts to have automatic effects, when God fully manifests Himself in you! Which is His Spirit.

Now that's deep and a level to aim for!

Get it in your head brethren! *"Christ like" Christ Like, Right living, and love living.*

Christ like, that's what a Christian is!

Going for God is being a Christian and it's actually a very hard and brave walk to walk and you have to be strong. Only the strong and willing can survive and endure the Christ like walk, allowing the power of God to move within you.

In other words walking tha walk with guidance from the Holy Spirit! Christians are "Christ like people", which is a 'title' to identify with "Jesus Christ".

I'm not gonna start getting into debates or some mix up, but it is people that make things complicated for real!

"If you are a Methodist, Pentecostal, Seventh-day Adventist, Catholic, Jehovah's Witness, Baptist or whatever title you prefer brethren, doesn't mean squat unless you follow what the bible (God's Mind) tells you to do (In Love) and by (The Holy Spirit) you are a Christian (Christ like people)! *At the end of the day it's all about Jesus!*

"It's All About Jesus!

I know it seems I keep repeating myself but let me clarify the meaning of a Christian to you one more time. By being basic about this, a true Christian has to be willing to be '**Born again**'? How? By living a new life, simply by not being a hypocrite or striving not to be a hypocrite at least, constantly putting on the new man (new character) keeping the old man buried (old character) I believe that's good enough.

'**Born again**' is being *'reborn'*, reborn into Christ. Coming back to your maker, God the father, taking on **Jesus Christ's spirit**, *'REJECTING SIN'* basically being *Christ like* again, being like **Christ**, acting like **Christ**, portraying **Christ's character**.

"Got It. Cool!"

God has spoken through people who have put His words and commandments in that

Holy Bible (God's Mind) why do you think God's presence was more effective back in the days.

In the **B.C's** (Before Christ) and **A.C's** (After Christ) people heard from God more clearly back then. There were no televisions, radios, newspapers, and magazines and the media didn't have as much influence at that time.

"On a serious note though", when you rewind back to the Old Testament, people were always praying to God, people were always repenting, sacrificing things to God and praising God, so God was more acknowledged.

"That teaches me that time period has kept on changing" coz we don't need to sacrifice lambs blood or oxen to God anymore.

God's presence was more manifested in the olden days. Actually in the Bible (God's Mind) it tells us clearly God spoke through Prophets and high priests back in the days, in the Old Testament days. Whereas now it's like no one gives a damn about God, the focus is drawn somewhere else, the world is so contaminated!

"Everywhere in this day and age come like "Sodom and Gomorrah".

"That's why God said, do not love the things of the world or follow the world, follow His Word and be led by the Holy Spirit.

I believe when Jesus came and changed the rules and set the new trend after He died for all our sins, it's like the world just went wild.

I believe people just started getting just a bit lazy with God and because the raw sacrifices and methods of things changed it were like; *"I can't be bothered to do things myself mentality".* The other excuses seem: *"Oh God has sent the messiah now and God won't mind this, God won't mind that, God is easy going, people over the years have got, just a touch too laid back and have taking God's 'Grace' for granted".* Well I'll bring it home to you again, Emmanuel's mercy is forever but God ain't foolish.

Jesus came! *'Yeah',* established Himself! *'Yeah',* will He come back? *'Yeah'!*

"So instead of letting the flesh and mind take over, let the spirit take over which Jesus left us with".

God speaks to us through Jesus now, not just through ministers, prophets, pastors or priests.

He (God) wants us to be like Jesus, coz Jesus is God's Character and mind.

Check out **Hebrews chapter 1** in the Bible (God's Mind).

We need to have *'Faith'* and carry out the promise, the authority and power we have!

The authority and power God Almighty has given us!

"Simple things we sometimes miss the point.

We get the people who do badness in the name of Jesus and God, and portray a bad example in the name of Christianity, giving Christians a bad name!

You hear about Christians killing, committing adultery. The majority of them exposed have been big *'so called'* *'Christian denominations'*, you hear about catholic and well known churches accused of molesting, raping kids, and coming out admitting they are homosexual and all sorts of madness.

The question is? *'Are these people'* actually *Christians?* The answer is no! You can't be a Christian if you are a killer, or rapist! You can't be a Christian if you keep wilfully committing a crime and you definitely can't be a Christian if you are a homosexual God calls it an abomination.

A Christian as I have said before is someone who is Christ like!

GOD IS NOT THE AUTHOR OF CONFUSION!

Christians and people who call themselves Christians that abuse the name always get exposed!

The disappointing thing is access is given freely to newspapers, magazines, television the whole media, to generate an excuse to mock God and make jokes imbedding that famous saying **"I thought you called yourself a Christian"** then you get fake Pastors, Evangelists, Reverends, Bishops, Prophets, Priests, Popes who just probably hide out trying to make a new life. Not practicing what they preach or know or fear God.

"They are deceiving themselves!

I say to the fakes: 'woe to you', if you are just in it to get a kick or career out of it. It's a big shame, but then again people make mistakes. The Bible (God's Mind) tells us about these people *"WOLVES IN SHEEPS CLOTHING".*

And more importantly people in general, tend to forget no one is perfect! Christians do sometimes make mistakes, but it does not mean that it justifies their actions.

I used to be one of those Christians giving Christianity a bad name.

"Yes I Teslim", was a *'So called Christian'* I would tell everyone, the police, friends, court that I was a Christian, but did things which were contrary to being Christ like. I was doing bad things, and demonstrating bad examples, claiming to be a 'so called' 'church goer' but I didn't know better. I was a bench warmer just going church for wrong reasons, basically for going sake, also as an act of respect which was not enough, but as time went by I learnt and I woke up and I did it properly.

See I was getting close to getting a relationship with God, my heart and motive were not too bad but my actions stunk!

People that don't care about God are in fact foolish and scared about commitment and are arrogant to submission! They don't want to believe, so they either criticise or eventually turn to something to believe in, or look for something to be a part of.

This ain't just my opinion it's true.

All those critics and self believers that don't know God, or have given God a chance or then again maybe knew God and then got sidetracked, discouraged, offended, or lost a family member, or went broke or, let some petty or minor thing that happened damage their lives. Lost hope, faith and just couldn't endure that walk and got shook and deceived. Or simply fell out of the boat, this can make people go a different direction, it happens, this however is how your strength and faith is tested.

The question is if you don't past the test what do you decide to do?

However you can pass the test with the grace of God! It says in **Proverbs Chapter 3 verse 5 and 6** *'Lean not on your own understanding'* your own 'mind' or 'self' but acknowledge Him 'God' and 'He' will 'direct you'!

We sometimes fail to recognise and realise there are reasons and seasons for things and bad things last for a season.

"Hold up, I'm encouraging myself"

'GOD IS GOOD'

Chapter 7

Atheists And Unbelievers

Ask these atheists and unbelievers what they believe? Their reply is normally what is God? There is no God. The next thing would be the IF, OR, WHY, WHEN or BUT questions. They say: "If God was God why this, why that, how did this, how did that, there are bible errors and contradictions, Jesus was a normal man.

"Why is it just before you cut of the conversation 'everyone establishes and agrees Jesus was someone who really existed, lived and may have performed miracles"! "Why do it to yourself and get yourself all worked up, mixed up and confused, for what?

People sometimes just want to mess up your focus because they are jealous they don't have peace of mind or focus so they try to mash up yours!

Not very wise! *DANGER* if you are not standing on the Word

(The Bible, God's Mind) you can easily be persuaded and conned for a while, that the 'Jesus' and 'Christian' thing is all a fake!

Happened to me many times in the past, that's why it took me longer to know Jesus. Do not be fooled, I repeat do not be fooled, don't let people steal your joy!

I was vulnerable and confused, in my early Christian walk then again I used to be a Muslim before I was a Christ follower and I realise now I never really had a right foundation or focus and belief in Christianity.

So please be rooted and grounded and speak the truth, never be afraid to retaliate in love and encourage in love coz these side trackers want to get you confused, so don't stand there arguing for hours our job as Christians is just to lay down the peace and truth foundation and give people an opportunity to also know the truth and gain peace so they can be blessed!

Why some people see people with peace and they want none is foolishness, everyone out there, needs to know greater is He who is in us than he who is in the world!

"That's God's word for the record!!

Not people or me trying to add and make up an idea of a God. *'FOOLISHNESS'* People are on assignments themselves as the devil's brothers and sisters some saying if God be God why don't He turn stones into bread, paper into money, metal into gold. What challenge is that? And what would that really achieve mate?

"Yeah exactly, nish. (Nothing!)

"Some people just don't give God the time of day".

I went to a place called 'Speakers Corner' one day, it's a place in Hyde Park Corner in London where there are tons of people, trying to get their point across about whatever issue they want to address. You could imagine the amount of beef, going on!

You would get the atheist crowd, Muslim crowd, black power crowd, White power crowd, racist crowd, new age crowd, Rasta crowd, equality crowd, human rights crowd all sorts of crowds.

Believe me 'brother' there was spiritual warfare there, heaps, of spirit of confusion floating in the air!

Anyways I just picked a spot with the crew and told it like Jesus did with my gun in my hand which was the Bible (God's mind) that is, and you could see the power, the Bible (God's Mind) generated by itself.

I remember two seconds after stepping in 'Speakers Corner' a black guy stepped to me and said: *"what's that rubbish in your hand, and why are you wearing earrings and rings and Gold?*

Then he kept repeating: *"are you a woman? are you feminine? Do you like men"?* As I was about to talk he said: *"why have you got gold in your mouth? Are you feminine only women wear so much gold on their body?*

I managed to keep my cool and smiled, coz I knew why I was there and expected this but not straight away, I knew I was on a ***"mission"!***

I told the guy: *"I am here to share the love of God and truth"*, and asked him: *"why are you trying to tease me? I am young and as far as I am concerned my earrings, gold rings, gold teeth is fashion and I like fashion, why are you trying to judge me by the way I look, Jesus never did that!"* Then he said: *"why does a Christian wear a big gold chain and have a gold tooth?* I said I was not always Christian I'm from the streets from road and God has changed me, I now have a relationship with God and He is going to use me as I am for His Glory. I then added: *"are you a Christian or Muslim?* He then replied: *Why? Why? "I don't have a religion, I believe in myself"* he replied out of ignorance, and said: *"there is one God but I believe in myself!* He then changed the subject and said: *"do you think there is going to be Gold in heaven?*

I said: *"yes heaven is going to be beautiful"*, he said: *"how do you know?* I said: *"God showed me and told me in His word"* he instantly said: *"rubbish!* In anger and then walked off, as he was walking off I asked him if he wanted me to pray for him, he continued to walk and turned his face to me and stuck his two index fingers up and walked on. I thought in my mind what an immature man I pray God touches and blesses this guy and may he know the truth!!!

This guy must have been in his thirties; he was also very smartly dressed and groomed, he looked like he was loaded.

I could definitely tell when I gazed into his eyes as we spoke he had no peace and he knew I had it, so he was trying to jack and strip me of my peace. He was too full of pride to even listen! Coz I wanted to give him the key to peace.

I know, that I know, that I know I have come a long way, coz if it was two years ago and he stuck his fingers up at me for no reason, regardless of who he was or where I was I would have attacked him and stepped in his face and probably would have attempted to rob him! Just to teach him a lesson. But I am not that same person anymore.

"GLORY TO GOD"

Anyways I continued to speak the love and truth at 'Speakers Corner' and could feel the power of the convicting words piercing through the air at the Muslims, Atheists, and other religions and crowds I walked into.

Different religions and crowds hated it, especially the Muslims and they would challenge God's words and the dudes would get more heated coz I would answer their questions straightaway by the Holy Spirit and opening my Bible. Boy that was training ground and a challenge for me, but you know what? I could actually see in their eyes they knew the truth; all they had to do was face it.

It did get a bit funny at times coz the Muslims would argue with me, and say how could I convert from being a Muslim to a Christian? I humbly answered and said it's not about religion it's about relationship. I told the Muslims that I know Jesus is the way, I searched for Him and He revealed Himself to me, most of the Muslim brothers would say yes Jesus is real but He was just another prophet not God. I would say I don't want to argue I'm here to show love. One way that love and peace was displayed was when Patrick, Noah, Zigfri, the crew and myself just sang praise and worship, worshipping God!

You could see everyone that was going by were touched or jealous? That there was a peace here coz we created an atmosphere and made 'Speakers Corner' 'Holy ground'.

I remember when I left I said I ain't going back to 'Speakers Corner' coz the spirit of confusion was too much there, plus no one wanted to listen, they would rather argue.

But you know what? I'll be back coz the fact of the matter is the Word is quick and powerful and I will decree again 'Speakers Corner' Holy ground!

Living this life of mine I have had a lot of experiences, I have knowledge about other religions, experienced conversations, debates and arguments about religion, but above all why do I choose to rely on God and represent Christ the King?

"Well I'll tell ya" Everything else I have listened to and researched has nearly appealed to me, but not quite like God *"Jesus Christ"* how He healed, turned water into wine, died for humanity's sin, mine included, God's mercy, God's forgiveness, the Holy Spirit, freewill and getting straight and direct answers from God by confirmation through people and His Word (The Bible).

"To be honest with you" every question I ask, He reveals and directs me the more I build my relationship with Him!

Come to think of it, even though I used to be a Muslim I still called on the name of Jesus to help me, sometimes by mistake, then adding Allah, and later in life finding out anyone can have a relationship with Him (Jesus) and it's not a white or black religion, or some mix up whether Jesus had blue or brown eyes, or multicoloured eyes, a afro, or had straight hair.

God can be any colour he wants "come on think about it", a real God can doing anything, none of this argument rubbish about if Jesus was white, black, Latino or Chinese, or if there was a 'J' in His name or not, obviously time period has modernised His Name Jesus, we are also living in a new time period.

Jesus name has been modernised between a mix of Greek and Hebrew. The Greek name for Jesus: 'Iesous', and the Hebrew: 'Yeshua', both have more or less the same meaning 'our salvation', He is just God and *I believe bro*!

It is scientifically proven that we all were made out of dust and we all have red blood, four fingers and a thumb, four toes, and one big toe, one mouth, two eyes, one head, two ears, one head, one heart, bones and all that jazz. These facts are the same with Jesus He is a fact!

It says in the Bible from *"The Beginning"* (Genesis) that God divided many nations in the 'earth' check **Genesis Chapter 10**, 'earth' meaning *"The whole world"* God telling us plainly, He divided and designed races and languages all over the world.

God is an artist, the best as a matter of fact, the best scientist. *Deep down I know it's true, we all know it's true.* As I said before God hides nothing, it's up to you to seek Him and build your relationship with Him.

Acts chapter 17 verse 26-28

I'll tell you brethren things are so advanced now days, I remember looking on the web site for the correct spelling of the ouija board thing, I just couldn't get the spelling right to find what I was looking for, so I asked about four people at work and they all said the same thing which was to look under witchcraft, so I did and to my surprise it brought up loads of witchcraft jazz and a variety of different religions and cults and what they get up to.

Some of which I knew about, suddenly I found myself going into all these things about bible contradictions, bible errors, atheists and cults all on the same page, man that's how you know certain things are not right especially when the truth gets exposed what a coincidence.

Everything I was reading and looking for was on one particular web page, all the topics I was searching for regarding witchcraft, atheists, cults and *what is religion'* stuff were all on one page, all sort of linked together, and all in a sort of agreement?

For some reason I started reading all this slander about bible errors, contradictions and so on and so forth, man! I tell you if I read this a year ago I would have been shaken and confused even more, and I would have probably not been a Christian now or pursued being a Christian anymore.

I feel I would have lost myself, because I took my Bible out and I was checking what the contradictions and bible errors were talking about, out of curiosity and shock, finding scriptures the site compared, analysed, and pointed out!

There were opinions claimed to be untrue and words and explanations given by this website to back up their point.

The Bible (God's mind) was being made a mockery of, this web site was basically saying the Word the Holy Bible (God's Mind) was a fake and stuff was inaccurate! Things such as what God said like, God said He does not lie or change, abuse about the Ten Commandments and hours when Jesus was crucified and that Jesus was committing a pagan act.

There were so much other subjects making the 'positive' and 'peace' look negative and foolish, which had me baffled for a few moments, but at the end of the day these are all stuff to deceive and confuse us and mess up our focus. I snapped out of the trance, which dwelt in my mind for a couple of hours and had me thinking, but the answer to this issue was plain and simple!

If you do not know God or want to know Him, you will not know the true answers, knowledge, wisdom, and understanding of His word, the riches of His mercy, His grace and blessings.

The bottom line is you will not understand Jesus so things will continue to be a blur, and mystery and you will not get an understanding or revelation of the word of God. Everything will sound gibberish to you.

1 Corinthians chapter 1 verse 18:

For the message of the cross is foolishness to those who are perishing.

The Bible is full of a lot of 'parables and proverbs', one needs to take that into account and overstand that!

Coz people are evil minded, wicked and self-centred they will look for things that can seem negative and mix it up some more. Coz rebellion and ignorance don't want to understand true wisdom, or truth, it's against God, it says in the word (Holy Bible God's mind) 'if you're not for God you're against Him'. You will never understand Him until you get to know Him (God)!!!

Just like a relationship between a man and a woman, or people forming a new friendship, if you don't get to know a person and you hear something about them or feel someone looks at you funny and they weren't, and they happen to be looking at something else, you will have all sorts of stuff to say about them, but take a chill pill *'get to know a person'* and see they are actually pleasant. "There's a saying that says don't judge a book by it's cover". Same with Jesus Christ you need to get to know HIM!

All these other religions I am going to mention below, I have to say a lot of them are confused or either lost the plot?

The Nations of Islam for instance their debates are just lots of "black this, black that, and brain washing. No route? We do need a good brain washing, but properly in that four-letter word L.O.V.E the love of Christ, love never fails. Did you know most of the religions actually believe there was a Jesus?

Yep the same one in the Holy Bible *"so what's the problem?* Yet you get all these other *"wrong beliefs"* and tailor made stories and disagreements such as Muslims, Buddhism, Sikhs, Hinduism, The Holy Tabernacle Nuwaubians, devil worshiper's, Harry Krishna, self-discipline, witch doctors, Rastafarians, many more that are not mentioned.

Unfortunately these are all cults, as a matter of fact the majority of Catholic, Jehovah Witness, Mormons, Church of England are also cults. Why? "Well any group that bends what Jesus is saying and use there own ethos, doctrines and get you sucked in as a member to follow their 'homemade rules', and 'control' your 'life' is a 'cult'.

'BEWARE' there are many cults around! Whatever the denomination it may be if they practice or do what I mentioned above they are cults, cults are *'life controller's'* so rely on the truth The Holy Bible! And be alert!

The book of **Timothy** in the Holy Bible (God's Mind) talks a lot about denominations and people with their own beliefs and doctrines!

Even the major cults i.e. the devil worshiper's know Jesus the Christ is the Son of God and are vex He is *GOD!*

Check it, Muslim/Islam, and Christianity are the two biggest, fastest, growing and most popular religions about. Does that not tell you something?

"Now, one God and one belief has got to be correct?

There needs to be one God, one focal point otherwise there is confusion!!!

Now the main differences between Muslims and Christians is Muslims believe Jesus was not God or the Son of God, but yet still, they believe He did walk the earth, carry out miracles, He did heal the blind, raise the dead, turn water into wine, and He was a prophet! Ignorance chokes the truth! The Muslim also believe if one turns away from their faith **(Islam)** to basically disown or kill that person! For the glory of Allah...

Their God?

"Now my friend that is not 'freewill', or 'love' or 'choice'. It is 'murder' and 'bondage'. In the Muslim faith you can't even question certain questions or answers, it is known to be a sin! The Muslim's say, it's only Allah that knows?

There are a lot of things wrong with the Koran. The Muslim's Holy book Qur'an claims to be the 'real deal' but yet the book states the way you earn your salvation is by deeds and works, yet the Holy Bible's emphasis is Grace (Unmerited Favour).

The Qur'an states there is no 'freewill' in their God Allah but 'control' of being a 'slave' to Allah. But yet the God of the Holy Bible offers you a choice.

The Qur'an links the Holy Bible into its claimed Holy book so therefore the Qur'an contradicts itself by teaching that the Qur'an accepts the Holy Bible and the Qur'an is in agreement with the Holy Bible but yet the Koran states different things about Abraham, Moses, Noah, Jesus and the Holy Bible.

That shows me Muhammad, the Qur'an and Islam are very confused. The Qur'an is a spin off, off the Holy Bible.

What Islam has done is add it's own philosophies on top of the Holy Bible.

The Koran contains many errors and contradictions in its own book! Plus the Koran is not in order, there is no clear beginning or end?

The Qur'an definitely is based on Muhammad's philosophies. I believe Muhammad was searching for God. Whilst searching, he tried to prove something. Based on his inadequacies and insecurities of lack of knowledge and wisdom he thrived on power so used that power to gain prophet status.

He has deceived many claiming to be a prophet but the truth is Muhammad is not and was not a Prophet. If anything he was and is a **false prophet.** There is no doubt he was a leader coz that's all he was.

Muhammad clearly copied Biblical traditions to base on his revelations in the Qur'an. A lot of people and Muslims do not know that one of his wives was a Jew and another wife was a Christian.

Another fact many Muslims don't know is Muhammad wanted the Holy place to be Jerusalem but the Jews and Christians did not accept his philosophy or religion so he changed his mind to Mecca.

Muhammad was a man of influence and power who gathered followers, to start his own religion called Islam.

Muhammad claimed angel Gabriel inspired the Qur'an, which was put together after he died by his loyal secretary. I believe Muhammad tried to follow the original plan of God in the Holy Bible but took it to another extreme to create his own religion.

"Well as I said before God hides nothing. More importantly Jesus loves and has given us all freewill!

Hear my heart again I'm not condemning Muslims but the truth sets you free brothers and sisters.

I was a Muslim my mum and dads were Muslims but we now know the truth!

The only good thing people who call themselves Muslim have these days, is a power, which will always work. God says it in

Psalms chapter 133 = UNITY.

I feel some Christians lack this area for some reason, but unity is a powerful force...

If we all got together as Christ like people, we would have a greater impact!

I feel all the promises and God's word in the bible would work more effectively, coz God says so, God's Word can also be used for right, wrong, good, or evil.

The Muslims and Jewish believe in most of the (Old Testaments) teachings but disown the (New Testament)! This is where it has gone wrong.

The whole Holy Bible (God's Mind), which is complete, needs to be followed.

"So I guess what I'm saying is the Muslim and Jewish are so, so close, almost there but not quite!

Take a moment to think about it? Who really says: *"oh my God Buddha, Allah, Rasta, elephant God, or self help me?* When you see a fine looking lady or car you know, what comes out by mistake or figure of speech is *"oh Jeeeeeesus!! Or Jesus!*

People call upon that name as a kind of signal to say: *"God that's great or nice or simply to say help!!!*

I reckon people are just afraid of peace, unity and one God.

People must be jealous that they were not Jesus or something. There are far too many Christian denominations and beliefs, I personally feel it's people confusing each other, messing up the real deal, the truth and main focal point who is meant to be Jesus, GOD!

We have the Pentecostal, Jehovah's Witness, Baptist, Catholic, Church of England, Protestant, Orthodox, Mormons, Anglican, Methodist, Seventh day Adventist the list goes on, these are all meant to be Christians (Christ Like People). God simply says worship Him in spirit and in truth and believe. Most of these Christian churches are just titles to suit their 'brand of religion'.

"Religion, religion, religion aye! A lot of people hide behind religion or use it for power or money!!!

I am not saying all of these is right or wrong, just 'beware', be 'alert', 'attentive', 'on guard', 'watchful', 'observant' all these Christians are all supposed to study one book (The Old and New Testament) which talks about Jesus.

The Holy Bible (God's Mind), personally I say do all what the bible tells you, to give you a tip the 'New Testament' is what to go by as the 'Old Testament' is for our reference, as we are all under a new law and covenant, and partakers of God's promises. So we are now in the law in Christ Jesus now! Not the old laws...

Simply study the bible, the New Testament is full of God's promises and you will know the truth and how God intended you to be!

The simple question is what would Jesus Christ do?

Some of these Christians titles/denominations I mentioned above don't even believe in walking in the Holy Spirit, Baptism, speaking in tongues, healing, prayer, Holy Communion, or worship. When it clearly instructs us to do that in the Bible (God's mind). And to think that is not bad enough you get the odd few *so called Christians'* making up their own rules, and doctrines for example the Mormons and their individual bible and confusion, delivering wrong teaching, teaching people you can have more than one wife *"yeah right!*

That is not what the Spirit or Holy Bible says, especially in the book of Timothy.

"Me (Teslim) I am just a Christian staaaaaaandard!

Born again, renewed, has faith, blessed and highly favoured, more than a conqueror, listen to gospel music and live by the Word of God that's me".

I'm not condemning or judging anyone but I feel it's not right to worship people, animals, statues, the moon or sun, images, objects, the dead, ancestors, plants, food, homemade Gods, carvings or yourself.

Listen guys there are real life people in the bible, people who have lived.

People that have witnessed the power of God, even scientists know!!!

I dare you to ask Jesus to forgive you, help you, and bless you.

"G O D smashed it you know", every single one of us, are created by God Almighty, He already lives in us. People like Noah, Moses, and John the Baptist are examples.

Many men and women are led in the Spirit of God and used as examples to deliver the right messages and the right path we should take.

"Okay some people ask why didn't Jesus live in the other people before He was born and when people didn't know about Jesus? More questions why weren't they born into sin? Well the truth is everyone was born into sin since Adam flopped!

Jesus has always been there, but awaiting His own appointed time to be activated as man, coz He is God.

Jesus was always there but He had to be sent as a confirmation and an example so guys like you and me can tap into the will of God the God of host. A point of contact was Jesus, who sticks closer than a brother.

Jesus came to prevail where Adam failed.

No one was ever born perfect or without sin! Since Adam and Eve brought sin into existence!

I'll tell you where sin popped up, that culprit Satan the devil. If Adam and Eve never ate that apple we would not have inherited a sinful nature, but they changed the format of things or you can say Jack and Jill or Mark and Louise, *"call them what you want 'Adam and Eve' are symbolic of the first human creation and we descended from them and they still ate the apple"*.

To my understanding Jesus to me is the Son of God, who is God and made Himself Jesus a son of Himself.

The only person who can do that is God!

I learnt in bible school once, that God had a perfect will and blueprint for us to follow and He planned in advance if we flopped, so Jesus is a result of that flop, not God's flop, Adams flop.

"You know something I would like to draw Adam to one side and poke him, and ask him why he messed up, and mashed up things, boy we would talk!

"Come on being serious, if God is God, the beginning, the end, the power fullest, the one that can see all things, knows all things, can do all things, can give you anything, can forgive, deliver, guide, be in any form He wishes, invisible, the head, He is gonna have a kind of P.A that's **'personal assistant'** to those that don't know what a P.A is I didn't use to know what that was until I was twenty.

Anyways getting back to the subject, to be able to communicate with God you need to know how to get in touch with him, that's how I feel about Jesus when I pray, Jesus the **P.A (personal assistant)** *"I say in the name of 'Jesus' because He is symbolic for son of God and powerful.*

Check out in the Bible (God's Mind): **1Corinthins chapter 12 verse 12-27.**

There is something about the name Jesus it carries efficacy, power! Jesus is the Son of God and God is in Him and He is in God!

Wow I just folded and unfolded a riddle for you.

In **Hebrews Chapter 1 verse 4** it says Jesus was given a big name, a name better then any other angel! Angels are the highest servants of God in heaven; Jesus was given a name above every name, a name that carries power! What a proverb, parable, riddle and clue!

Jesus begat Himself, wow He was God in flesh! I feel that's deep! When we tap into God He taps into us.

I remember in my early Christian walk, I used to be baffled as to what kind of relationship Jesus had with God? It seemed very close, but as I got to know God I later found out Jesus is the big G O D manifested in the flesh!

People have asked me in the past God might be a he or she "well to cut the long thing short, God is God, the word 'He' and Jesus refers to the same thing in the Bible which is Jesus! Also 'he' and 'man' is the head, as we all know as 'dominant', its funny and deep.

God did not come as a Juliet instead of Jesus. Society even know a man is *"thee boss"* the head of the family, man was created first and all have bigger, stronger bones than women so that's why people like me and Christians refer to God as 'He' sometimes although 'He' has many names, I won't even go into all that jazz. But the main thing is, God is Almighty and He is SPIRIT.

A lot of people from different religions have tried to confuse me in the past, many of them I have agreed with in the past but not anymore. They can try and hinder and discourage me but I can no longer be shaken, my feet is planted in God and I now know Him too well now, to be shaken.

"All I know is, Jesus said He is the way the truth and the life! Capish! No ifs no buts it's true. "Please, leave the foolishness on the floor!

People say there are so many questions, and mysteries about Christianity, but then again, there are also a lot of clues and knowledge about Christianity, if one bothers to pick up that awesome book (The Holy Bible), you will see for yourself. Ask the scientists they even know that the Bible (God's Mind) has many truths in it. They have been researching and discovering a lot of the events in the bible actually did take place.

I believe in Jesus and have a heavy relationship with Him, everytime I talk to Him He answers, when I pray in 'Jesus name', and I do what the Holy Bible says it always works?

Why is it when I resist the devil he flees?

Why is it I had so many problems and when I decided to walk right as a Christian they have disintegrated?

Why is it everytime I pray, prayer works?

Why is it my relationship with my parents is now good?

Why is it I never lack? Why is it I am always safe?

Why is it the Principles of the Bible always work when I follow them?

Some people say the Bible (God's Mind) contradicts itself. Okay so why is it so accurate when you study it and obey what God commands!

I keep repeating this but if you only get to know God, His mind, His word, **'parables'** and **'proverbs'** unlock and reveal revelation to you. As I said before the Bible (God's Mind) is full of **'parables'** and **'proverbs'** I challenge anyone to follow Jesus, and do what the Word says, especially the commandments I bet you my life it will work, actually I won't bet.

"Lock off", I guarantee it will work! If not email me and call me a liar, I am living proof. God works. Remember to take things one-step at a time and don't rush. Knowing God is a *'process'* the more you seek Him the more you develop.

I have seen and learnt when you do what the Word of God says and the more you live right you will be a witness to the things and promises of God, coz when He says He will do He definitely does!

When you feel you are down in the dumps, God has got your back, when you are hurt, God has Got your back, when you feel you can't hold on any more, God has got your back, when you think you have lost hope, God has got your back, when you feel you are broke and drained, God has got your back, how do I know? Coz I have experienced these things and have found God was on the case He had my back, He came through for me.

His Word is true and powerful! I ain't just repeating myself, I'm giving you the key, and I want you to catch the point! *"I am not just telling ya, my Spirit is! And that Spirit is God. Plus on top of that, let me give you a tip off, when you're bang on doing God's 'kingdom business' it will be a hard battle, coz loads of flashbacks from your past will try to attack your mind, trying to distract you from overcoming and moving on. It's like something constantly tries to block your righteous walk.*

Remember "it's all good", you've just got to be strong firm and alert, basically keep prayed up. Coz the devil again is on the case he tries to make you sling your hook, he knows you will be powerful when you know who you are and when you are aware of what authority you have in Christ Jesus. The devil enjoys attacking and playing with your mind!!!

The devil is jealous of your promise coz he ain't part of it!

So what am I going on about? Well I'm just letting you know you are not just a conqueror you are more than a conqueror and you will make it, continue sowing seeds down to the smallest things such as cleaning someone's car, house, washing up dishes, speaking life (Good Words) the more blessed you will become it does not always have to be money, coz sometimes no one has 'no paper' (cash money) to give, your act of love shows you're a server, your brother's keeper, walking in the Spirit.

"You better be real and trust in God no matter what!

I want to say, if only you're willing, 'just willing' it don't matter what sin you have ever committed or what is haunting you, or what people's bad thoughts about you were, or what was said about you, forgive them and pray, even if it is just a one minute prayer. God will forgive you no matter what you have done even if you think you're living right, now, and think your sin is not a big sin, it's tiny, don't be foolish sin is sin. God ain't stupid just acknowledge your error and sin, and repent straight away to God the father Jesus Christ!

Forget the old things, if you got pregnant, sold drugs damaged lives, cheated on your partner or hurt someone just bring it to a place of repentance. Free yourself!

God is a forgiving God, a God of chances, a gentleman, no strings attached, no gimmicks, no hype, God said it and He will do it, He is not a man that He should lie. That mighty guy Jesus died for your sins and mine.

Just activate your faith and lean not on your own understanding.

WITHOUT FAITH IT'S IMPOSSIBLE TO PLEASE GOD TO GOD BE ALL HONOUR ALL PRAISE ALL GLORY

Advice: *Realise the devil is the prince of the air and we need to take charge of the atmosphere by the Word of God!*

Advice: *We walk by faith and not by sight!*
It's not about religion it's about relationship!

Advice: *The Word can be so simple that it can seem too simple!*
HAVE VALUE IN PEOPLE.

Chapter 8

The Spiritual Realm

It's a supernatural thing that God does when He uses the things that look, seem, and sound foolish or dumb for His glory!

What the so-called wise and knowledgeable people think is foolish, God uses, example people like 'me', the 12 disciples, and water turned into wine, wow! "I say what's the point being a *"pain in the backside all your life"*? *"Glorifying yourself then going to hell*?

Wisdom is better than silver or gold.

"Oh you think **HELL** is **FAKE** okay go on carry on", *"with that self knowledge and evolution mentality" "you're on your own mate"*

There's a saying you know: **If you can't hear you must feel!** *"You feel me"*?

Why do I rely on Jesus one hundred percent? Hmmm, that is the question, why? I rely on Jesus coz He transformed my life and my spirit!

I remember seeing a ghost in a form of two men who both blinked about twice and then suddenly disappeared in front of my face, I was 7 years old, now that was an experience I'll never forget.

How did I know they were ghosts? Well they both suddenly just appeared for about *30* seconds and disappeared in front of me, when I screamed. They were detailed men and yet see through? 'Strange' isn't it.

When you finally get the guts to tell someone, a friend, family member, scientist or a so called specialist about what you saw or what took place everyone seems to try to fob you off and say: *"oh it may have been a figment of your imagination"*, and try to tell you, you were tired, freaking out or going nuts! Or try to convince you, you were dreaming or something. And you end up confused yourself nearly, coz people make you more or less, deny such a thing took place, it's like *"don't be serious"* this cannot have taken place.

Sometimes people's opinion don't mean nothing coz **'you experienced'** it and saw what you saw. Ain't nothing gonna change that fact!

What we forget is titles and professions don't actually realistically mean squat! When it comes to a circumstance like this, coz they are human just like us, who have studied in a profession as a doctor, specialist, scientist, counsellor or what ever the profession. The deep thing is man can't comprehend what is seen if it is an abnormal thing, especially if it is extraordinary or supernatural coz the human existence is used to what we consider the norm and certain things we see in movies that seem to be unreal. If we actually experience something similar, unusual or extraordinary, a human being sometimes can't handle it!

So society tries to make up excuses for what really happened or what took place, and tell you, you must have been experiencing some sort of tiredness, daydreaming, confusion, shock or something?

Movies and television actually give us a lot of clues and exposure of truth. But again people fail to see what is happening coz they don't want to accept the truth.

THE SUPERNATURAL AND SPIRITUAL REALM IS REAL.

I am definitely sure it was a big, big challenge, the disciples of Jesus Christ were faced with, when they watched Jesus walk on the sea, and when they saw Him vanish into the clouds. If you were to see a man floating on air besides you, you would be shocked!!! But that is 'supernatural'.

No one would probably want to believe it, even if there were witnesses, coz it is out of the norm, and certain human beings just can't accept or face facts!

When I saw that well-known magician David Blaine or whatever his name is levitate in the air on three occasions, I was shocked but believed it.

Again some people may have seen it and just thought no, that ain't real!

Just an illusion, but what is really an illusion? Did you know an 'illusion' is a vision or an image too! *"Don't be fooled"*, there is a spiritual realm! A lot of things we see that society tells us are not real can in fact be real! *"Don't be fooled"*...

'Magic' is real and magic means supernatural and magic can also mean unexplained! When you look into magic, you cannot explain a lot of what happens in the supernatural, the spiritual realm. There is not much difference between MAGIC and TRICKS!

These are the devil's main weapons he uses on us 'magic and tricks', which are artificial things, deception, lies and destruction.

My brother you have got to question what is behind this? What force?

My brother it's 'demonic' trust me, I'll leave you to research the facts and the root of how this magician David Blaine does what he does. By even watching it the people laughed and praised him, if they knew what was really taking place they would not laugh at all. *"Coz it ain't funny trust me!*

"Guess what? In Christ we possess a power greater than the devil's power! That power is 'Dunamis and Exousia power' which means 'supernatural power' in Greek, that power comes from God, which He has put in us by His Spirit. That's why God says all we have to do is resist the devil and he will flee. After all God created this joker called 'Satan' so therefore He has given us authority over the devil and any other joker working for Satan.

Such as witchdoctors, voodoo priests, obia and devil worshippers, this **'Authority and Power'** is only available in and through **'Christ Jesus'** so tap in!

When I was about *14 years old* I took part in an Ouija board game. People normally pronounce it (weji board) a witchcraft demonic game, which I played in a French class lesson in secondary school. I now call it *"foolish fun"*. I can remember everything like it was yesterday. It was a French lesson and an excuse to mess about, coz most of us including me didn't have the patience to learn the language. So our class totally fooled around in French class.

On this particular day we took advantage of the tutor, we went about it by taking it to the next level of disobedience, *"maximising foolishness"*.

Our French teacher Mr McConville was always soft, but this time around he lost his patience, and got fed up, so he locked us all in the classroom and said he would be back with the headmaster.

We always used to play a game in our French lesson so we started debating if we should play bingo or hangman in English instead of French, before the headmaster came. It was the last lesson of the day so we relaxed.

We all decided to play something new, scary and challenging and whoever *"chickened out would get rushed in the corner"*. (A class beating)

We all came to one deep conclusion just like that, the conclusion was we would contact our ancestry spirits and the dead. So we switched the lights off, drew the curtains, and two Chinese boys began to draw and make the ouija board, we used an empty bottle as the dial and began the game by spinning it. It spelt out a short name, which we all presumed meant nothing. It spelt 'Ian', and there was actually an Ian in the classroom at the time, which happened to be my friend, he was laughing at first and didn't think anything of it at this point!

Someone wrote everything the ouija board was spelling on the black board for us. Everyone started to take it in turns to spin the homemade dial including me. Nothing was really happening for a while, when the bottle was spun, it just kept pointing to people.

Then it spelt out 'Y' and then the next spin was 'O' then 'U'. It spelt *"you"* when we spun the bottle again it smashed on the floor and suddenly everyone began to speak, fooling around and laughing saying, who is here? What is your name? It was a joke at first, but it started to get serious, coz the bottle had smashed *'so everyone thought okay a bit creepy?'* We continued by using a plastic bottle for the dial and spun it again. It spelt another name, I think it was 'Sue' then when the bottle was spun again it did not stop spinning, it continued to spin longer than usual but everyone thought it was a joke and was trying to laugh it off as a joke but the truth of the matter was it got a bit freaky!

Everyone watched around the table then the plastic bottle dropped, then suddenly we all watched a ten pence coin move on the homemade Ouija board in the mid darkness of the classroom, two paces by itself, with about twelve other people around the table. When that coin moved everyone in that classroom *'screamed and jumped'* and was silent for a minute or two, holding each other in fear, because we were all scared! 'FACT'...

The teacher had been absent from the class for about twenty-five minutes by now.

The windows and doors suddenly started to make a banging noise; nobody wanted to believe the Ouija game caused the noise. Someone switched the lights back on, myself and a few other boys ran to the door to get out, but the doors were locked and nobody came, even when we banged and kicked the door.

A lot of my classmates that witnessed what took place all said they felt an *'unusual cold presence'* experience, it was like we triggered different spirits in that room, some boys and girls were even crying, mainly the boys.

When our French tutor came back it was way past the end of the French lesson, it seemed like a mini detention, we didn't even complain we were relieved he was back, we just all wanted to break out of that class room, he unlocked the door and we all sat down like 'excellent students' in fear! He didn't even say a word he just wiped the black board and let us go. Then we all got up and ran out. Ian looked worried and some people thought things might happen to him. Thank God nothing seemed to have happened to him.

What an end to the day, after school everyone stuck together because some class mates knew of people who had died playing that game!!!

When I think about it now, *"it was nuts"* playing that game. We all knew some information and discussed the danger about the Ouija board before we started the game, but no one in the class wanted to look like a *"Big fat chicken"* or they would have definitely got a rush in the corner. That night I went to bed with the covers tight over my head *"believe"*...

"For your info if you're not clued up as to what Ouija board is? It's a witchcraft game, a game which people have died, been cursed, haunted and possessed by playing.

It's a game you use to get in touch and invite familiar spirits, believe me you cannot contact your dead relatives, what you actually do is invite demonic spirits that try to deceive you and posses you. It works! I would strongly advice people to stay away from this sort of game! Would you believe they sell this dangerous game in innocent well-known toy stores such as *TOYS R US'* that's *"liberties"*...

I mentioned earlier that I have seen a ghost, I have also got another experience to share with you. I have seen a manifestation of something that look like a little demon getting bigger and closer to my face. I have seen some weird things man. You might say what is a demon? It look to me like your typical demon image everybody perceives a demon to look like, I would agree that it was an image of a typical figure of a demon coz it also had elements of that description in the Bible, in the book of **Revelation**, a beast with horns like a goat, fangs, sharp teeth, ugly goat kind of looking thing. "Anyways the saga was" I couldn't sleep one night, I was 18 years old at the time and I saw this image twice, if you want more detail it was red and had two horns, my brother has seen something similar too.

"Maybe that experience was because I was buzzing, high off the ganja that night. I'll let you draw your own conclusions.

Weird init?

Chapter 9

Why Do I Have A Belief?

What is belief? If you asked me personally why do I have a belief? My instant come back would probably be: *" I just believe in it! "I have faith.* But after swiftly researching what belief means with my thesaurus gadget thing and dictionary I can express it further to you, coz if I didn't I would be talking so much slang you would be mixed up yourself. So it's a good thing to bring clarity straight to you, you get me?

Belief in my own explanation is *trust, love, faith, confidence, assurance, principle, expectation, guarantee, security, passion, conviction and a challenge,* which are all connected to *belief,* these are also the tools we are automatically entitled to and need as *"a believer" "a Christian"!*

I wake up every morning praying and immediately after, loads of thoughts enter my mind and I have to battle! One, I don't feel like going to work, two it's like I feel what is life all about, three, time is running out, four, am I worthy of living, five, how will I make it, when will I make it?

But you know what I have to make that strong choice, which is to be positive and have faith, focus and believe. And see the clear picture, that life is a challenge, I'm gonna make it, God will help me, I don't need to be shook, I have to stand strong and remember I am more than a conqueror, I am forgiven, I walk by faith and not by sight. I am highly favoured, God has given me authority and power over serpents and scorpions and spiritual wickedness in high places. No weapon formed against me shall prosper!

I have a goal a purpose a *belief!*

I must remember there is power in my words. *"Hallelujah my words carry power"* so I have to kick off and don't get too trigger-happy but speak positive vibes! By speaking life! I can't get side tracked and let the enemy (Satan) play with my mind and have the upper hand and throw all this negativity at me and try to mash me up.

I must unleash positive vibes and mash him up, this is war and this is where I can get trigger-happy Banging up the devil!

Now I have that belief, gained that focus my eyes are open, I see things for what they really are. I can see there is a supernatural world and a spiritual world; my spiritual sight has kicked in. That crap called 'vanity' is removed from my eyes and I can see clearly not letting the cares of the world hold me down.

I don't just see physically, worldly and carnally but I see beyond normality a gift we all can activate if we want to.

Belief is Faith, in God's word, which is The Holy Bible (The mind of God).

Pain or Peace?

God It sometimes hurts man! When I see loads of lost people day in day out. Totally lost and without the peeeeeeeeeeaaaaaacccce, lacking a focus and a belief.

I personally want everyone to also have a belief. And have a revelation of belief. A belief in Christ, Christ that means the Anointed one, anointed one that means appointed and chosen one, who is Jesus, I, you, if you want to be? *Anointed that is?*

A belief that offers, focus, integrity and peeeeeeeeeeeeeeeeeeeeeeeeeaaaaaaaaace!

Please repeat this peeeeeeeeeeeeeeeeeeeeeeeaaaaaaaaace!

Say it again peeeeeeeeeeeeeeeeeeeeeeeaaaaaaaaace!

The word is nice isn't it, feels nice and sounds nice! I'm just simply asking you to speak this into your spirit!

I truly believe when you finish reading this book you will be able to identify with the peace today for the first time or again. The real peace, peace from God Jesus, the peace you have always been searching for!

A lot of people have missed the point! People are constantly searching, left, right and centre, searching for what? We all know what *'PEACE'* but sometimes people end up going around and around and around, in huge circles and constant dead ends, something I persistently did for a long time.

Searching for a peace in money, sex, women, fame, relationships, house, cars, jobs, clubs, liquor, and drugs? I really, really thank God I got delivered from all that mess and gained *'a focus'* and peace! *"So can you", my friend!*

What you need is right here, right now God, Jesus the Bible (The Mind of God).

Are you gonna get caught up in the fire? Fire burns and when it burns it hurts!

John chapter 14 verse 27: PEACE I leave you, my peace I give unto you. Let not your heart be troubled, neither let it be afraid.

John chapter 15 verse 15: Please read all

Romans chapter 5 verse 1: Therefore being justified by faith, we have PEACE with God through our Lord Jesus Christ

Ephesians chapter 2 verse 14: For He is our PEACE, who hath made us all and has broken down the dividing wall between us.

Philippians chapter 4 verse 7: And the PEACE of God, which passeth all understanding, shall keep your hearts and minds through Christ Jesus.

Chapter 10

The Thief

He is on a mission to deceive, steal, souls, minds, hearts, and kill.

John Chapter 10 Verse 10 read this scripture in the Bible (God's Mind).

The sad thing is our eyes are blinded and don't tell me this is rubbish or some kind of holy righteous talk thing. Satan, Lucifer the devil is real. And he is out there to keep you away from the peace, truth and the benefits of it! The devil wants to be glorified at all times and wants to be ruler of the earth. Which will never happen!

Satan is the biggest and fattest saga setting, catastrophe making, sleazy undertaking, deceiver making, thief taker, shabby, dusty, shady trickster and hustler.

The devil was thrown out of heaven coz he wanted all the glory and all the power! That's where he flopped, this dusty devil served God in heaven for a season, as a worship leader! Worshiping as an angel amongst angels, which did not please him anymore, so he tried to do his own thing! Remember angels are created just to worship and serve God!

This is where I believe God went all out and told the devil *"sling your hook"* and dashed him out of heaven and that's where the devil began his evil kingdom on earth. Kick starting with Adam and Eve!

The devil is on a constant mission with his army of demons seeking whom he can corrupt and destroy and bring into hell to serve him and be a part of his evil crew. Yep hell is very real! The devil and his demons are real! If you chose to go to hell, that's what you will probably end up becoming, a demon? Where on earth do you think all these films and horror ideas come from, good or evil?

The devil is also known as abaddon, accuser, ancient serpent, angel of the abyss, apollyon, beelzebub, belial, coiling serpent, dominion of darkness, dragon, devil, enemy, evil one, evil spirit, father of lies, gliding serpent, god of this age, leviathan, liar, lying spirit, murderer, powers of this dark world, prince of demons, prince of this world, red dragon, ruler of the kingdom of the air, tempter, shatan and Satan.

The devil's name was also Lucifer, which means "son of the morning". He was the most beautiful angel created, and the man in charge of music, so don't be surprised by Satan's skills, and how music is today because it has been corrupted a great deal today and influenced by the devil (The mischievous one).

1 Peter 5 verse 8: the devil walks about like a roaring lion seeking whom he may devour (demolish/batter).

There are a lot of clues in the world all day long. Where do you think all these horror movie ideas or anything displaying evil comes from?

"Where do you really think it's from?

Definitely not inspired from the Holy Spirit. *"Do me a big favour and do a little analysing and research for once in your life".* You will see more clearly trust me. Then you can tell what is real and what's not.

Why would you think someone that has killed, robbed, sinned to the max and not repented would just die and that's it?

Get a grip that's not it my friend, we have something called our soul our spirit that lives on, our bodies are just houses of flesh where our spirit lives in!

Our body is what God calls our "temple" which He wants Righteous and Holy and which we all know rots away.

My friend, I want you to please let go of that rusty mentality if you were to die today that you turn into a butterfly or something. Coz my friend that's not it, you will go to Hell or Heaven. And it would be never-ending torment in hell.

Hell I believe from some of the things it says about it in the Bible (God's Mind) is definitely extremely uncomfortable and irritable it would be like a knife constantly going in and out of you. Feeling that pain of burning every second wishing you could just sleep or die again, but can't and nothing to sooth you or ease the pain, instead you would probably be gallivanting around trying to suppress and attack people as a demon to get the pain and torment off your mind.

"But on the other hand there is Heaven, it is peaceful, Fun, Beautiful, no pain, no fret just paradise. Which one will you choose?

God has given you choices *"Life or Death" "Blessed or Cursed"* it's up to *you!*

God can't make you choose, but desires you to choose Him and have life, and have it more abundantly!!!

If you have never taken the opportunity to ask God for forgiveness of your sins and accept Him as Lord God almighty and activate the Holy Spirit in you while you have the chance. *"You are going somewhere worse than Freddy Kruger's nightmare"*!

Trust Me!!!!!!!

CHOICES?

Life is all about choices; God gives us so many opportunities to come to Him (God).

In the Bible (God's Mind) He says He does not wish for anyone to perish, but some people may love sin too much and though we may get drawn and caught up in it, God will still call and invite you to *'His glory'*. He may strip you of everything you value to see if you seek or ask Him, so He can help you so you can enjoy the benefits of His **gift**, His **love**, His **promises**, and His **peace**.

After all He did give His life on the cross as a living sacrifice for my sins your sins, everybody's sins why? Because there was sin in the world and man has a sinful nature, which came from Adam. But guess what? God came to take away sin to give you grace and fulfil scripture and prophecy in the Bible (God's mind) so He came as man Jesus into the world, so that you may have life! To be able to get in heaven with God you must have no sin in you. How can one be free of sin? We are not perfect?

This is where Jesus stepped in, He came to give His life as a living sacrifice and took those sins from you and me and left His name, blood He shed on the cross and lifestyle as a promise of purity so that we may accept Him. To be able to dwell in Him and with Him when we are on earth and when we leave the earth, with the ease of knowing He has paid the price for our sin and made us perfect again in His sight, so all we have to do is fight the fight of faith and righteousness and be grateful He did that! And inherit paradise and peace in heaven!

He wants us all to worship Him and believe in Him by declaring that He died for our sins so we can identify and operate in the Holy Spirit, which is Him God, so that you may have life! Literally a good life!!!

If God never did that, as far as God is concerned we are born sinners from the descendant of Adam so we would not be able to enter into heaven coz we would be full of sin and not pure.

So the carnal and natural soul would just be cast away into hell, as there would be no Holy Spirit! But Jesus loves us all and we are His creation and He chose to purify us again and give us a choice if we want to stay in that purity, that pure nature which He has made available.

So what's it going to be? Life or death blessed or cursed?

Talking about chances briefly everyone gets a chance to give their life to God almighty. If I were you I would take that chance *"quick"*!

All these voodoo things, black magic, witchcraft, curses, and these things are reality but a lot of people think it's a bit of harmless fun or a joke! "Yeah you keep joking".

I dare you look into it. Not only did I know of people who practiced witchcraft, this thing is common, and all around us all day long but eyes are blinded so people fail to notice it, coz people are busy chasing vanity!

All these evil demonic things are 'blatant', palm readers, physics, tarot card readers, mediums, witches, devil worshipers, there are even advertisement in newspapers promoting witchcraft. There are also people you least suspect involved in witchcraft, some of those are in power, politicians, musicians, celebrities, and gangsters, practicing witchcraft and demonic stuff, drinking blood and all that jazz.

"Deep init, it's a fact mate! Wake up and open your eyes".

You may question it's harmless and it's not your business "well would you mind your kid or family member getting caught up in any of that crap?" I feel you would mind and would most likely like to prevent it!

But why on God's earth would you let a psychic or medium determine your future anyway. They most probably will determine your future, and most of the things they say will happen to you, will happen, coz they are possessed by a demonic spirit of evil who is who? "That's right" the devil, who can lead you where he wants if you let him. God speaks love! Plus *"words carry power"!*

God said it, wake up and smell the 'coffee', if one is not for God, Jehovah, you're for satan the devil and he will lead you in the perfect will of his ways, he is the master of deceivers so you will hear what you want to hear, and see what you want to see.

For example, this palm reader dude would try to map out your future, it's always meeting that stranger tall and dark! What stranger?

"Demons my friend! You will find love in a man or woman you meet, yeah the wrong man the wrong woman more like, what you really will find is lust upon lust, sex, abuse of your temple and no peace.

What happens when corruption meets corruption? Destruction!

You are often told you will get married, *'DANGER'* married to the wrong person more like, and then you will probably divorce, a soul tie will brew up here or you will be bound in depression.

"Boy when you marry someone you both become one". It's a deep supernatural thing, you both surrender your will to each other, what did I mention earlier, words carry power. When you both openly declare, *"I do"* it's another kind of ritual or a ceremony but a legal and moral thing, an agreement, a declaration to the atmosphere, God and the world basically!

The upsetting and dreadful thing is if you marry the wrong person you're *frigged.*

These so called psychics even tell you the key things too, such as be careful, some one is going to try to destroy you! But what happens again you blatantly ignore an important warning, you're so excited and miss this part of the information.

What you have now done is given access to an evil spirit to speak into your life and spirit. *'DANGER'* Then you're told you will find fortune, done! Signed to the devil and possessed too!

As a matter of fact when you enter into a presence of any of these familiar spiritual things either paying or not, you have automatically sold your soul to the devil.

What you've done is open your spirit up and let a familiar spirit dictate to you words of influence and corruption.

The only way out is if you genuinely repent and get delivered and walk in the right will of God!

The deal is you will find, it a bigger challenge to snap out of the dilemma coz you would have probably found wealth and false pleasure

'Pure vanity' and peer pressure. You just come to the point where sin is too sweet. But also know deep, deep down something still ain't right, something is missing.........

There is no such thing as perfect looking women or men, but people have images and ideas that they assume will provide happiness. A media and society point of view, regarding men with the six pack, a great body and women with the perfect breasts and body.

"No such thing brethren! Things can look good but nothing is perfect!

Have a real hard think and try to figure out what is really *'perfect'?*

Only God is perfect!

Now back to the subject on getting delivered from the thief (devil). Getting back to God to get delivered will almost be impossible coz you went down that road and got yourself caught up in a trap!!!!!!

"Selling your soul to the devil" is deeeeeeeeeeeeeeep *mate!* There are lots of ways to do that!

Even without knowing, that's why you need to be careful when you're having fun, you can be leaving your mind and spirit open to anything and everything. You might wear familiar objects, do a strange sacrifice, swear your life away or on something or get involved with undercover witches, or blood rituals and all that jazz, carry on and you will be promoting the devil.

Just coz you want to get something that comes and goes, money, wealth, fame, relationship, women, men, sex, the list goes on and on. You can fall into a trap!

In Africa, India, the Caribbean, Haiti and poor countries where there is a lot of violence, struggle, poverty, famine and killing. You tend to find witchcraft, voodoo, juju, obia, black magic, sacrifices and evil doings more blatant!

Demonic and familiar spirits are more common and raw in these countries, coz there is not as much television, or idolized figures such as celebrities and false advertising, but everyone still desires what they don't have and would do almost anything for, things such as money, power, sex, women, men and wealth.

People even steal or kill so they can go and pay to see a witch doctor to gain wealth or power or carry out a sacrifice, something like their blood or go all out and just simply make a pact with Satan! *A soul sold a done deal!*

The deceiver the devil is everywhere all shapes, sizes forms, in make up and glamorised, besides everyone seems to want wealth, love, sex, money anything appealing to the flesh. So the devil hides the bad points, just like we have for example Casper the friendly ghost, Harry Potter, these are false influences especially to little kids who watch this crap! But these things don't seem too harmful coz it's been presented in a good package almost making *REBELLION AND WITCHCRAFT* seem normal?

The core of these things is evil, witchcraft, rebellion, and demonic.

There ain't no friendly ghosts they're all the devil's army of demons. People assume evil things or spirits always come in a form of an angry big, bad or scary image, this is not the case, they also come in cute, nice harmless appearances too mate.

The devil comes as an angel of light!!!

There are a lot of demonic books, films, and cartoons out there constantly trying to attack and corrupt the new generation.

I don't even condemn those people that write those books, films and cartoons because there is a spirit behind it, the inspiration does not come from good, love, or the wisdom of God.

Just like I have been led to write this book by the Holy Spirit of God, an individual that writes about demonic, evil, and violent things such as books, films, and cartoons without warning, advice, exposure or teaching of a lesson to expose the dark side to a story, are being inspired by demonic and evil spirits floating around the atmosphere that's where they draw their inspiration from. If the motive is to share an entertainment of fear and not entertain love, the 'Agape love' (God's kind of Love) it is wrong. It's easy to get drawn in, not that all films, cartoons and books are bad, the majority of them just give a negative story and a bad influence to society to fight, kill, get revenge, cuss, sleep around, party, get drunk, get high and be a hero, the true hero is Jesus Christ! If you check it, He always gets a mention when someone is in trouble.

If you are not exposing the devil or evil, you are promoting it.

I suppose because I am exposing a lot, I don't have fear but, *"my guess would be"* Satan is angry about what I am doing and writing about, and he will try to hinder and attack me in all different ways. Which he tried physically, the night after I finished typing the paragraph about selling your soul to the devil and this actual paragraph, starting: '**Satan is angry**' and ending: '**all different ways**', two lines up.

This was actually Christmas eve of the year *2001* by the way, It was about 5am in the morning I was still sleeping then suddenly opened my eyes, it was dark and I was laying on my side and moved to lay on my back to get up. As I looked up laying on my back with both my hands on my side I felt my neck tightening up and my head felt like someone was pulling it back in a position to slit my throat, so I tried to move my hands and just get up and pray coz it felt like there was two big hands wrapped around my neck trying to strangle me.

I was really irritated, and scared and wanted to pull off what ever was around my neck, or even just touch my neck, but the thing was, I couldn't even stop what was happening I felt paralysed, the only thing I could move was my feet. I couldn't even close my eyes or speak either, my mouth felt gagged up, plus I couldn't breathe properly. I was so vex and suddenly I was aware something demonic was trying to attack me coz it had happened twice before but not like this, this was a bit tense.

I really wanted some help here and wanted to call my mum but I always locked my room door so it was a bit of a challenge.

"You know something, this torment was happening for about *10 minutes* this time".

It felt like something was trying to suck my breath, energy and life away bit-by-bit.

I really did feel like I was slowly dying *'on the real'*.

I now knew what was happening, so I just calmed down and started praying in my mind and said: *"I resist the devil in Jesus name"*, I couldn't actually move my mouth to say it!

I was prang, shook, *"I was in some mix up,* I just kept on praying pressing in then slowly my mouth felt loose, so I started praying out and then I finally rose up in shock jumping out of my bed and started speaking in tongues *(speaking in the spirit)* and punching the air saying: *"Satan where are you?* "Satan is a liar the devil is a liar", and I just laid there resting, smiling, thanking God. Saying: *"Satan is a minor all I have to do is resist him and he will flee. He has no power over me!*

Then I sat on my bed, shocked at what just took place then laid on my bed for a few hours, I didn't sleep though, coz I was still shocked about the saga.

It felt a bit weird? When I decided to tell people, I felt people would look at me like some punk, or twisted, only to find out other people and friends had experienced it too. You need to get militant with him! Show that demon who is boss!

"Greater is He, that is in me, than he that is in the world!

"And Greater is He, that is you, than he that is in the world!

What is that Greater thing in me or in you?

That Greater thing is He, who is the Holy Spirit? Jesus, God. And at the name of Jesus every knee has to bow. That name Jesus carries power!

"Say it, Jesus, say it with authority, Jesus, it does not even matter how you say it, it's still powerful anyway! **Jesus, Jesus, Jesus, Jesus,** I love that name Jesus; I think I'll name my son Jesus. Why not it's a great name don't you agree?

The devil tries to stalk us but we have to stay in the Word the Bible (God's Mind)

The devil is real, and I'm exposing him and I don't care. Guess why? We have power over Him! AMEN,

READ THESE SCRIPTURES:

James chapter 4 verse 7: Submit yourself to God. Resist the devil and he will flee from you.

Luke chapter 10 verse 18 – 19: I beheld Satan as lightning fall from heaven, Behold I have given you authority to trample on serpents and scorpions and over all the power of the enemy (devil).

God's Words says: The weapons of are warfare are not carnal but MIGHTY in the pulling down of strong holds.

Chapter 11

Secondary School Days

My brother Michael landed in London, on the last year of primary school.

He got the same treatment as me, born in London, shipped to Nigeria for a while to learn the culture. It was heavy when he came, I was happy to see him coz I was lonely. He did get on my nerves though, we had a typical big brother little brother relationship. He started primary school and then a few months later I started secondary school and we just kind of started drifting apart from there, coz I started changing.

The journey began as a teenager!

You know something *"changing"* the subject briefly I don't know why my parents just didn't let me do certain things. I probably would have calm down more instead of always being *"on it"*, and rushing to find out if I was really missing anything, every chance and opportunity I got. Anytime I did get the opportunity to play out I always over done it.

"From experience I feel when kids don't get the freedom to play or be a kid, they are always curious, and feel as though they are missing out on something, most rebel when that happens it's true".

When I started secondary school it was an exciting step for me coz my best friend Hainsley Dickson was also going to the same secondary school. When we started we just drifted apart, he done more hanging around his cousins and girls. I supposed he forgot about me first.

The secondary school I went to was one of the worst schools in south London.

"Cutting tha long story short! I left my first secondary school, coz of three reasons. One, it was rough, two, I got suspended, once, and might have got expelled, coz I got caught scamming dinner tokens, and finally three coz of two boys.

Two of the older kids that were known, to have a reputation of fighting and causing trouble, one day called me, these boys always tried to lure me in their little crew, coz I wasn't "on it" they tried to always rob me when I bumped into them? They were always trying to rob me, for money, but I never had none, so they picked on me anyway.

Hainsley weren't around to back me up, we were in different classes and he stuck with his cousins.

Anyways one day I was skipping, class and unfortunately I bumped into them, they both pinned me up, against the wall and one jabbed me with a needle.

They jabbed my arm once, with the needle and laughed running off which hurt and made me feel a bit woozy.

In those days, sniffing glue, solvents, black markers and heroin, were the in things to get high on, cannabis was not as easy to keep quiet, and sometimes get hold of, plus who had the money, so I'm sure the boys who jabbed me with the needle were probably high at the time, they were definitely on something.

That needle probably had heroin or some kind of drug in it. I was so vex and scared, coz I never had anyone to turn to, such as family or cousins in the school.

I wanted revenge and was afraid to tell the headmaster, so I told my mum who then told my dad, that's when I changed, schools and landed in my new second secondary school. I felt different in this school I was the shortest in my class. All the older lot in school called me a nickname that stuck to me like glue until I left secondary school. The nick name was 'ant', the girls called me it, the boys called me it, then sooner or later I found myself graffiting it everywhere, again my focus was messed up, my desires were girls and fun.

I really disliked the aaahhhs, your cute, you sound cute treatment, most of the older girls would call me cute, I disliked it a lot it really irritated me!

This secondary school my parents thought was good, was worse and still is one of the worst schools around today. Not blaming my parents, they had to get me into a school, and they were told this was a good school.

This school was meant to clamp down, the amount of sex abuse, abuse, drugs and violence that took place in that school. My mum and dad again were not happy with my behaviour, which meant I got beats.

I messed about in class, I stole exercise books, library books, and stationary and all that jazz.

My parents didn't know that I was stealing everyday, and that I felt I had to, coz I was hungry, because other kids always had, but I never, so I got it in my own way, which was wrong!

I believe my parents couldn't afford it at the time, but I thought they were being hard on me. I started scamming dinner tokens again, and there were others that also did it, so I didn't feel too bad.

The in things *"back in the day"* to make money off, was breaking into cars, stealing car mobile phones, and car stereos. I didn't take part in that department, but I made money in other ways. Which was stealing chocolates and sweets from the sweet shop, near my secondary school.

I was so good at it and I was never suspected, I would take orders from most of my classmates and steal them their order, and then bring it back to school and sell the sweets and chocolates for cheaper.

Other ways I would generate money was when we did sports, about two other classes were having their (P.E) lesson It was called practical education, so I would sneak into the changing room whilst everyone was out doing sports and would have that idea in my head, whoever got on my nerves out on the football pitch would *"get it!"* Or anyone that even, slightly irritated me, I would pretend I was going toilet, then head for the changing room, walking the long way around, so it looked like I was not heading for the changing room toilet.

When I got there, I would then go around the changing room searching and going through peoples belongings, I would take peoples money, it felt like pay back time to me, I didn't care *I was just concerned about me, myself and I.*

I would do it to about two or three people's belongings and fix there belongings exactly how it was, so it looked like it was untouched. I took their cash and stuffed it in my pants, oh yeah back in those days they were Y fronts (pants) where it stayed. Classmates mainly realised at break or lunchtime their cash was missing. When some did realise, when they finished changing, in the changing room, the teacher would search everyone's bag and would tell the class that they are disappointed with whoever did that. And if they were caught they would be suspended. Meanwhile the *"scash money"* was hidden in my Y fronts.

The teachers would never take responsibility for any money missing and they always made it clear, as it was too much hassle for them before and after a lesson.

When I did this changing room thing, I wouldn't go to the shops stealing orders, instead I would go and buy a nice sandwich and play arcade games. It would be a nice lunch, and a home time snack, buying something I liked, plus stealing something I liked at the same time. It was a routine and a bad habit I just couldn't give up. I always got what I wanted. I got used to it and it became the norm to me, it seemed very harmless as I did this despicable thing.

I also never, ever got caught in the changing room doing what I did, but often came close, a few incidents as I started searching someone's pocket or bag I would hear the door opening so I would instantly, style it out, by pretending to take off all my sports kit, then go to the toilet and sneak back out, it was a big risk coz if I ever got caught by any of the school mates I would have got a good old rush by everyone.

When some people used to find out their belongings were not how they had left it and found their cash missing, I was always the first to tell everyone to search me and suggested everyone should get searched.

I thought I was smart, I actually thought I was. I always did get away with it though. *Every thief always gets caught eventually!* You always get caught! No matter how long it takes or how good you think you may be.

I actually remember getting caught once! *"Stealing!*

One of the story goes like this. One Friday at secondary school, my friend Darren who's house I sometimes went to, to watch porno films, and play Nintendo games, kept provoking me, by teasing me, calling me all sorts of names and making an example out of me with his different swear words and name calling lingo. He used cuss words, that were explicit, cuss words under the sun, that were very filthy, in front of about twelve people who saw and laughed, making me feel "small" like a big fat punk!

It was so embarrassing and I couldn't make a come back. It came to the lesson before lunchtime. I was on "pay back" mode. So I went to hang my coat up purposely next to his. As he was busy messing around, I started to pickpocket his jacket, to take all his money. Then discovered he had it in his trouser pocket, so I went through his jacket some more and hit the jackpot.

I got his keys that meant without his keys he would be locked out of his house coz his mum gets back home about seven. I then pretended to scratch my neck and neatly dropped his keys down my jumper and smiled as I walked back to my seat.

During the lesson I felt content, and started to laugh and joke with Darren, and started to think what should I do with his keys. Should I just throw it on the roof? Then I came to a conclusion, I always wanted more games for my game boy I had stolen previously from a classmate. I was never suspected or caught for that one though.

I stared to think about what I should do with his keys, I knew Darren had loads of game boy games, suddenly bingo! He was a spoilt brat, he had all the toys a kid would want. I made a decision right there and then in my head, I was gonna go to Darren's house at lunch and steal his game boy games out of his house. It was lunchtime, everyone was at the adventure playground, near school, and was having fun, we had about thirty-five minutes left for lunch.

I pretended my stomach was really hurting, and told everyone I was going to the medical office and might go home.

I faked it so much, two friends escorted me to reception at school and left me there, *great alibi! "Wouldn't you agree?* I made my way to Darren's house, it took me about fifteen minutes, when I got there it took a while to unlock the door coz there were three sets of keys on his key ring, when I got his door opened I was gonna take his Nintendo, but it was too big, he had so much things I wanted in his room. So I took his game boy instead and all his games, I stuffed his game boy down my pants and turned his room completely upside down!

I went into his kitchen I turned on all the gas on the cooker, and then knocked over all the flowerpots and bins in his house to make it look like someone broke into his house, then took all the spare coins in his piggy bank.

I left his door wide open with the key left inside, then rushed back to school. On the way, I emptied out his game boy case and accessories on the street and stuck two game boy games down my pants, and put three in my bag.

Anyway I felt good when I got to class, Darren started to be nice to me for some weird reason? He asked me how I felt, I did feel a bit bad for messing up his house though, but I got my own back! If he wanted to carry on taking the *"Berties"* it was fine coz I had his game boy and game boy games down my pants.

Over the weekend I sold the game boy for ten pounds and gave it to my mum, I told her I found it and she was happy.

Then Sunday afternoon Darren's mum called my house she said did I know who broke in their house? Coz her neighbours said they saw a short black boy that fit my description, trying to force the door open. My mum listened to every call in those days so she butt in and asked Darren's mum what the problem was?

To cut the long story short, we went to Darren's mum's house. Mum, dad, brother and me all four of us. When we got there, Darren weren't there, his mum was explaining the situation and said out of the games I showed her, two of them can only be bought in America and explained Darren had those games. Then she said if I say it's definitely not me she would call her neighbour and police to take it further. My mum then asked if it was I, I said: *"yes!*

Then my mum *"sparked me"* and started shouting, that slap connected on my face and hurt so I started crying, my dad said when we get home I am gonna get punished like never before, and I fully believed my dad, he mentioned something about putting hot, hot pepper in my eyes, my mouth and in my back and bottom after he beats me, and give me a mark I will never forget!

Anyways I was scared and thought "bomb that" so I pretended to go toilet and I opened the door discreetly and ran out of Darren's mums house, I planned to run away from home that day, and never go back! I got to my good friend, Menelik's parent's house, and his dad called mine and persuaded him not to beat me. I got favour! Menelik's parents dropped me home and his dad persuaded my parents to just talk to me. So I did not get whooped! *"Thank you Lord"*

It's a bit funny to think I used to walk into shops, blatantly with a belt strapped around my jacket, grabbing goods in bunches and filling my jacket up with bottles of Lemonade, ice cream, Twix, Marathon, chocolate bars now called Snickers, and several other popular chocolate bars and sweets.

I was so good at it, I looked at the shop assistants and always new where all the reflecting mirrors or cameras were, coz I scanned them as soon as I got into the shop. Any shop was a walk in a park, I even stole at the same time, I spoke to some of the shopkeepers, I would pretend to cough or sneeze loud for a while, to "style it out" so the noise was unnoticed as I stole their goods.

If I was stuffing large amounts of crisps and chocolate down my trousers, I would tuck my trousers into my socks, and wrap the belt round my coat, I call that raw stealing.

I would drop about fifteen chocolate bars, ten packs of sweets, down my trousers.

I stole for my friend's so I could get a free smoke, at fourteen I lost my usual crowd of friends since the incident with Darren, so I hanged with two white boys called Ian and Stephen. I always got high on drugs with them, at lunch times. I also stole loads of goods for them coz I never had the money to make up for the price of the drugs we bought, I always got my smoke and high which felt cool at the time so I felt like I owed them something.

Ian was a bad influence and he was such a pervert. I remember when all three of us went to his girlfriend's house to take it in turns to have sex with her. Sick now thinking about it even though what we planned never happen, coz her grandmother was there so she told us to come back the next day.

Ian was always boasting of how mature he thought he was, by trying to grow a beard, how much drugs he smoked and claming he had sex with older women.

I was just such a little thief. I would pick up items from every shop, stall, market I entered with the intention of stealing something. Any and every shop I went to, got it!

I got chased about twice, in three years but never got caught. I got advanced in stealing, I would use so many different methods. Meanwhile my schoolwork and studies was neglected, I started skipping class, and I couldn't even read properly no more.

I was even branded dyslexic by some teachers, and told I may need special help, but that was not the case. I think I just got lazy and forgot a lot of the things I learned and my mind was on other things, my interests blocked learning effectively.

My mums always used to say I was silly because, I played the scapegoat, because I was little. She always said, I should stop playing the fool and act my age. And compared me with other kids suggesting to me, why I shouldn't do this or that.

It's like she never knew what I really got up to but it was like she could read me and basically, would have a rough idea of what I was getting up to, but not say nothing coz she was not sure. My mum would always kinda, judge me due to the fact of past incidents, such as when I got caught by a security guard stealing a hand held game thing, which led to my headmaster having to get me and then my headmaster calling my mum and dad. That was the first time I was banned from a shop but it was far from the last.

Secondary school days, those days were something else, when I look back on secondary school I had so much fun it was pure fun. Especially the science lesson, I always made stink bombs with sulphuric acid and many other chemicals. I can remember playing with fire all the time, nearly setting the place on fire, many times with the Bunsen burners I would also roll A4 paper into cigar look-alikes and smoked the paper when the teacher slipped out, a few of us did that.

Our science tutor was strict but he could never handle our class, we were the second worst class in the entire school Mr Kashani, was his name, I feel sorry now for all the grief we used to give him.

We always knew how to push his button and he would always burst out swearing using the "f" words and called us "little bastards" we used it against him too every time he said he was going to get us suspended by the headmaster or give us detention.

Mr Kashani was having a fling with one of the female tutors, one of the teachers that loved playing badminton after school, so everytime in science "biology class" as we talked a lot about sex education, we would bring that up and tease him asking if he had sex with her in the school changing rooms after school. He would be embarrassed and tell us to "f-ing" shut up, "I guess out of major frustration and call us "little bastards" again, under his breath.

Music and social and careers education was another one I remember, that we did absolutely nothing! We did nothing in these classes but mess around or bunk the lesson, which meant not even turning up for class just simply skipping class to go and smoke. *95%* of the time we messed about in music lessons but some how we always put something together and performed, this is how I found my drumming talent and ability. *I love the drums and I love rhythm.*

French, R.E (religious education), and geography I really disliked them I just couldn't take in anything the teachers were saying. I found it so boring the only fun times were when the original teachers were not around and the supply teachers filled in.

Maths, History and English were the only class in which we were kept under control and learnt coz the teachers were very firm they had everything locked down they didn't take any crap!

I remembered when I urinated on one of the maths teachers after school by mistake. I was doing my thing on the wall near the school reception and suddenly, the teacher came round the corner and walked into my pee, it was all over his trousers my friends started laughing and we started running, than God that teacher did not say anything.

My favourite lessons were P.E (Practical Education sports) and drama. At school through to college I was always noticed and popular. I was loud, excited and one of the shortest kids. So I always felt I had something to prove.

I moved out of South London as my parents thought it was rough down there and a bad influence, which it was and we moved to West London.

It seemed like countryside, down in West London, it was different and seemed to be more spacious, the air even smelt different.

I didn't know anywhere or anybody. I missed South London. I always went up there. I soon couldn't be bothered coz the journey was too long. So I made new friends down west and stole, smoked and slept around there instead.

So much people were jealous of me for some reason, actually coz I boasted about being from south London, so I got beaten up a few times, I remember getting stamped on my face till I was unconscious and could not move anymore, when I got home I looked in the mirror and couldn't even see myself. I was huuuurrrrrrrrrrrrrrrrrrrrrrrrt!

It was hard getting revenge coz all my friends lived in south London and if I dealt with the beef drastically how I wanted in west, I would be in "drama by myself in west. As time went by I found I couldn't trust anyone in west coz they never had my back when I got into "beef.

I started to get familiar with west London and started seeking revenge, I got CS gas and occasionally caught a culprit by himself that rushed me, and fought back. *Anger and rowdy time Activated!*

Chapter 12

Church Days

"I remember going to church not knowing God properly but going to church mainly because my parents did. When I was at church I would watch and laugh at people who were Christians, and think 'what's this crap about?

This clapping, shouting and singing rubbish, I was like what are these 'funny duddy' people doing, their nuts. I used to be amused at Christians dancing, speaking in tongues and worshiping I thought it was all a joke. Most of all I thought it was fake.

I even used to sing dirty songs in church whilst praise and worship was happening and got caught twice and got slapped twice by my dad. Which hurt but still continued to do it, coz it was not of interest to me.

I remember one particular service I was so bored I went to the shop.

That particular day I had my dad's car keys in my hand so when I snuck out to go to the shop an idea popped into my mind. I thought why don't I drive my dad's car to the shop, so I got into the driver's seat of my dad's Volvo the car was parked directly in front of a pole, I put on the seat belt and saw an old friend from primary school, so I decided to show off, then put the key in the ignition and I started the engine.

I had never drove a car before or had a clue what to do. I never knew that automatic cars moved straight away when you put it in gear D so I put it on gear D and pressed the accelerator, the car smashed straight into the pole. I was scared all I saw was my old friend from primary school laughing and smoke oozing up from the bonnet, so I ran out of the car and ran all over the estate looking for someone to help me fix this thing.

To cut a long story short I was very blessed my dad didn't beat the crap out of me, I think he was too ticked off!

Imagine if I never had the seat belt on, I would have definitely gone through the front glass of that car windscreen; I was so fortunate God was around coz boy the impact was hard.

I thanked God that night that I didn't get beats, all the ministers and elders in the church just kept on telling my dad to calm down and don't worry about it, I'm glad they intervened coz I was dreading going home.

Church was always a waste of time to me. On Sundays all I wanted to do was go and play out with the boys. I sat there every Sunday in church biting my nails and falling asleep in service.

I went to church every Sunday with my parents, knowing what I know now, my parents were still Muslims. I think my dad really believed or had faith in Allah coz of his mother and father and family. Coz there were not around he had the freedom and breathing space to find his faith and belief it seemed to be heading towards Jesus so whatever dad said my mum and the kids had to do also. As far as he was concerned he was the head and man of the house. I personally thought the churches my parents began to go, were old-fashioned churches. First it used to be those African old-fashioned ones where you had to take your shoes off and wear a long white cloak.

I call it the "the white gown gang church". You would see everyone in long white gowns women in long white gowns and huge white caps, "mind you, I went to a church like this one twice or more in Nigeria, they did some funny things and to tell you the truth I hated it!

Then as time went by we ditched that church and forgot about those white frocks and went to a normal church, which seemed much more down to earth, it wasn't though. It was actually full of gossip, envy, jealousy and people demanding power and respect not love. It's funny what you suss out when you're young. You see a thing that ain't "correct, that's why one has to be careful how you behave round people!

At this church they would just talk and go through the Bible in zero love, it was of no interest to me. The only thing at that stage I looked forward to when going church with my parents was playing the drum kit and making music, which we all know as 'praise and worship'.

I had to sing at the same time my parents did, everything always seemed like a task or rule in relation to the *"church thing"*. When I went I was always told to dress a certain way, how to behave, how to greet the elders, how to serve, but certain things were right but the way 'certain things were done were just a bit over the top. That put me off church *a lot* every Sunday to me was just a routine. That was the idea I had about church as a kid, you see I didn't get any solid foundation at the time. No excitement and no character was built.

Playing the drums in church meant nothing to me, but fun. It was like I was in a music lesson at school, having freedom to express myself, despite the fact! Of the anointing hitting me a few times, but because I was not really a believer for myself, nothing changed.

I believed because my parents believed.

Little did I know I would become a worshiper too, an usher, evangelist and counsellor and clap my hands and dance like it was the last time I was ever gonna bubble and glorify God Jehovah, knowing Allah is a fake, a moon god and Mohammed never rose from the dead only Jesus did!

Thank God for meeting Curtis, Million, and Jenny, who took me under their wing and showed me the way, coz they allowed God to work through them!

"I am now always in a hurry to get to church."

Chapter 13

From A Criminal To A Christian

When I was fifteen, I stole a gold pen from a well-known stationary shop, that was my first arrest.

I stayed in the police cell for about five hours, I was so scared I thought I weren't ever coming out. It was my first time being arrested and handcuffed by the police, my mother and father were not happy, I will never forget "that one slap" my mum delivered to me outside that police station!

I must admit we get it easy out hear in Britain and Europe with the police, if it was back in Africa, America or the Caribbean, the police would buss your face, the beating you would get before you were released is some punishment and a half, the feds don't pet out there, they're would probably even shoot you dead.

I left secondary school with crap grades grade called unclassified, G's, E's, F's and all that jazz. I just about, made it into college to do my drama course. My parents were not happy I was doing drama, but that was all I was interested in, so it was okay coz I convinced them I was retaking my English and Maths and would pass this time. "College days, man it went quick, I done so much clubbing, smoking, and more stealing, I had two big fights, once I got sparked in the face and just sat down coz I actually felt guilty stealing this guys mobile phone, while playing black jack, the other fight was over a girl.

I always stole from the shop near my college, but only for myself, everyday. I even stole from our canteen, coz it was easy everything was out in the open.

Then I found my new making money scheme. I got giving fake twenty-pound notes and fifty pound notes to change into real money. They were good ones they look so genuine the paper was good too. I would go far, skipping lessons to change it, into real money, it was so easy for me, I started buying the fake money of a brother that supplied it. And change it so I could make the profit for myself.

I made so much dirty money off it, I only got chased twice, once in McDonalds, KFC, and a sweet shop. A petrol station tried to lock the doors and call the police, but I managed to force myself out and ran off. I started to sell fake fifty pound notes, and tell people how to use it and distract people in shops.

I remember going to a well-known fast food restaurant in Piccadilly Circus in London. Where I changed a fake fifty-pound note to forty-nine pounds, in real money. I did it for two weeks this Australian woman was working at this place and was just taking the fake money? I bought a pizza for one pound every day for two weeks and this lady didn't have a clue? I even took people up there to do it for me, three times over, so she wouldn't see the same person three times.

When I could not be bothered to go up there, I would sell the fake fifty pound notes to students, and guarantee them they could change it there. "Until it got a bit hot, and the restaurant found out, coz I think she got fired! I spent that money on my first Armani cloths, designer shoes and my first mobile phone, and all the rest of it.

Sooner or later that scam ran out coz I had travelled everywhere to change fake money and everywhere I tried to go back to had the pens to check fake notes, so it got long (waste of time). I remember stopping a man in Richmond, London, I asked him for change for a twenty pound note and he gave me two ten pound notes, and stuffed the fake twenty pound note down his trousers pocket, that seemed to be a good way to start going about changing the fake money but even that got long. So I stuck to gambling.

I played fruit machines gambling thirty to sixty pounds, sometimes winning, sometimes losing. Then in college I would play black jack for money. It got to a point where I started to skip class to win my money back coz I got greedy. We would always play blackjack for £5 pounds a game, I cheated sometimes and made money, soon kept losing and owed people money. Things were going down hill again I got suspended from college for a week coz of a mobile phone incident. And found myself on report for two weeks.

I just about passed my course, but failed my English and maths again and I was not accepted back in that college to take further courses. I wanted to take the second part but was not accepted back in, so I had to find another college that would accept me. I didn't want my parents to find out I couldn't get into college. It was hard coz my grades and qualification were not enough to get into the course I wanted to do.

All I had to do with the time I spent in college was work hard and attend all lessons, but I messed up again. It seemed like nobody wanted to accept me. So I lied, about my grades and my name. This is where the string of aliases of names started.

It worked, I got into a college and the course I wanted to do, but there was one problem, I had a fake name, fake grades, fake qualifications, so I got a fake driver's licence, then a fake bank account, fake everything! It all seemed to be a big fake but I chose to carry on.

At this stage of my life I wanted to prove my parents wrong about their thoughts about me and succeed in my own way, but amongst the fake names and scams, I got sucked into the wrong crowd yet again, and started not just stealing small things but bigger things. I got involved in robbing people for large amounts of money, the target were businessmen and laptops!

I remember one of the few robberies that went wrong, I drove and followed this woman, on the bus she got on, to her stop, then one of the guys I was with jumped out of the car and pulled the laptop of her shoulder.

She wasn't having it, so another guy came out of the car and punched her in the face coz she struggled, with her laptop, and then we got it. As I was driving off, a black guy came in front of the car to 'play hero' so I sped up, trying to knock him out of the way, it was like a movie coz as soon as we did that, when I got to the bottom of the road there were three police cars and I was driving fast, but they were busy dealing with a situation to realise what was happening.

The victim somehow got my number plates and the police came to my house the following morning and raided my room. They took me to the police station and kept me there, trying to make me talk so I got a good solicitor and every answer I gave was "no comment". That arrest nearly landed me in jail for three years, as I attended an ID parade but got off the hook! I felt untouchable so I carried on with robbery, I was just interested in making quick money as I got used to a flashy lifestyle mentality!

To think, up till this day, the guys that were involved with the robbery that I thought were my friends wanted to shoot me over a silly misunderstanding. They thought coz I got away with it I named names.

I took the wraps for this crime, I had to go to court to explain why I was driving without insurance, licence and tax, and I got banned from driving and a fine.

I kept on driving but would get caught again, I got caught about five times driving on a ban! When I went to court the fifth time, I still drove to court. That day at court I met other criminals that were passionate about crime. And one day I met up with one of the guys who I dropped home from court a week later.

We met up and went to rob a well know pizza place! We went there with two long kitchen knives and crept in through the back way. We thought there were two people there so we both grabbed a person each and stuck the knives to their throat, unfortunately there was one loose cannon an extra person who screamed and jumped over the counter and ran to the door.

We forced one of the men to open the safe, but it was dry, there was nothing there so we ran off coz the third man had got outside shouting for help. Imagine if I had got caught?

I smoked weed and drunk excessively trying to escape reality, and live my own tailor made reality, like the rap stars did. I tried hard to get a job and landed one in a well-known fast food restaurant as a cashier. I made my own money while I worked on certain burger promotions I stacked pennies up near my till and would press the [No Sale] button, and give customers their change and made money for myself. I would always make about thirty to sixty pounds for my self at the end of the night. My till was never down but was always over, when my managers cashed up my till.

I soon got fired, not for getting caught, but for turning up late.

Imagine if I had got caught?

I did the exact same thing at two other companies I worked for.

Imagine if I got caught? *"Imagine?*

I got to the stage where I had no job, and I "sure was not working in a fast food place again, or anywhere I could be seen coz of my reputation, so I signed on for benefits, free government cash. I got kicked out of my college, smoked my brains out and drunk myself silly.

I started going church again on Sunday's coz I was searching for peace and felt a bit guilty, but I was only a Christian for the day. I was not a genuine Christian. I just wanted peace so I started playing the drum kit in this new church I attended by myself.

I started going *"out there" by myself, "out there"* meaning making moves going to find something or someone to rob. I went into banks looking for who drew out the most money so I could rob them. I remember bumping into my dad once and was lost for words, but I managed to make up an excuse.

"God I was such a thief! I wrote my tasks down daily, things such as what I was gonna steal, stuff included silly stuff like ten tooth brushes, five soaps, fifteen cd's, Champagne, food and drinks, clothes maybe a new pair of trainers, a jacket to sell, a pair of trainers, rob someone worth robbing, clubbing, then having sex with someone different. Wrote all these mad things down!

I stole petrol more than twenty times.

I bought stolen goods to sell on.

I was a typical bad boy that I'd always wanted to become.

I actually believed in my own laws!

I felt like I enjoyed life, coz I was always buzzing high, waking up late, sleeping late, and clubbing twenty four seven.

I got drunk most times before I went clubbing, so I *"enforced rowdy time"* which was thee motto, so if I got into a fight I wouldn't feel a thing! The amount of cab drivers my friend and I beat up were countless, *God forgive me!*

My typical day and life went something like this

This is what I Wrote On Paper once:

17ᵗʰ Monday go job centre sign on (for benefits free money)

18ᵗʰ Tuesday probation.

19ᵗʰ Wednesday community service.

Steal wire, soap, tapes, batteries, and cds to sell.

3.30pm pay court fine.

Buy some clothes, Armani glasses, get Gucci shoes this week

Get some fun tonight

Hair cut, Buy a quarter of weed (marijuana), Get £100

Get credit card numbers

One day it all just came on top and I broke out crying in my room, loud in anger and frustration! I came back from community service upset coz I was working for free as my punishment from court.

Upset coz I actually felt like a criminal, vex coz I was being ordered around and being put on report. I hated it. I felt like I was in jail and I felt suicidal, my parents came up in my room and saw me in a state screaming shouting! I kept shouting: "I just wanna die: "I hate myself.

I was now searching for peace and more or less God, and could not seem to find it! I was bound by community service, probation orders, trying to get out of court, consequences, and avoid jail.

I tried to avoid court and community service once, by not turning up, coz I was fed up! Once again I was caught. Like one day, the police stopped me and my name was checked out, it turned out I was wanted for assault. I was arrested and detained in the police station cell, yet again!

The amount of times I had to report to the police station, getting handcuffed trying to beat the system, fighting the law were countless! The headache, was getting too much, I got away with crime so much, it was catching up on me now. I was now, getting caught, and getting worse!

I got stripped searched so many times "what an embarrassment and predicament! The police would put on their rubber gloves and tell me to pull my trousers and underwear down, I ain't saying nothing bout what happened next. It's too embarrassing man.

But then God stripped search me and arrested my heart, now we both tight! God is now my Crony, my best friend, and my brethren! Did you know God calls us brothers too? **John chapter 15 verse 15:** God calls us friends.

"One thing though! I had some principles when I stole I never stole from friends and family, I knew and was close to, the only friend I ever stole something from was Darren.

I was such a violent person, and got a kick out of hurting people. I would just get uncontrollably drunk and high and start causing chaos, beating anyone and everyone in sight up! Intimidating people, it was silly I know but that was then!

I once, dragged a man out of his car and punched him up, one time coz he kept slowing down for no apparent reason, I did so much senseless things like that man, I got drunk just to cause major destruction and act out nearly all the rap verses I heard, and idolised at the time. I enjoyed listening to the rapper DMX back then. I shared a lot of his pain and I felt he related to my life and what I was going through.

My stealing habit got worse and worse, I got to a point where I didn't steal anymore coz I had to, but to prove I could, for leisure, challenging my own self? I lived my own reality of being on a high, I would have two hundred pounds in my pocket and still steal senselessly it was a habit! It was a normal thing to me the mentality in my head was " I was just getting mine", my own way.

I remember walking into Oxford Circus in London, I took a blade with me and cut off the alarm on a expensive jacket and bought a cap then walked out with a brand new jacket. I took a fresh blade to many other designer shops and I would do the same thing. The same shop in Oxford Circus I stole the jacket from, I went there again and tried on my favourite trainers and put my old ones in the box and then walked out casually then caught a bus!

Then went to smoke with friends and get a haircut.

I sometimes did spend a lot of money on clothes though. I always had a little hobby of stealing cameras with film in it and enjoyed walking around with my camera everywhere taking pictures, my little own idea of being creative. I found it was fun especially when I was drunk back then, I took many explicit ones too, sexual acts and all sorts. I am surprised up till this day that the local developers developed such pictures.

Double Trouble

My friend Matthew Carty brought him to my house once, for a smoke and we got on!

Then one day on my stealing spree I bumped into him. His name was Damian Broom, we were in a big well-known music store. I started chatting and then told him it was easy to steal cd's in this store coz I knew where all the cameras were and who the undercover security were. I stole about six cd's to sell and he stole two.

"Double trouble" "We clicked"!

We hung about together for the whole day, I didn't trust anybody in west London but I found that trust in Damian.

We done so much together, you name it, the motto was: *"getting on rowdy"*, we would be getting drunk, smoking, raving, clubbing, orgies, stealing, stealing car parts, jackets, games, trainers, shoes, phones, robbing people, car jacking, stealing petrol by filling up and driving off, taking anything we could get our hands on.

We were a bad influence on each other and could not be separated. The amount of times we got chased by the police together and got away was countless. It was funny when we went to Pizza Hut once, we ordered and left without paying! we thought things like that was hysterical.

We were involved in two major car crashes, the first one was like a dream, I was racing a old college friend I had not seen in a long time after just stealing a new car battery for my new car, and as soon as I crossed the junction a Honda smashed right into the passenger side door which was Damian's side.

I suddenly found myself driving on two wheels firmly controlling the wheel then the car dropped back down and I sped off. It was a quick hit and run, funny enough we got caught and detained in the police station for four hours but nothing happened to us they just let us go.

We broke almost all the laws, in a way we lived by our own laws, scammed the trains, buses, taxis, liquor shops, cinemas, petrol, shops, designer shops, clothes, benefits, sweets, food, people, some clubs, to think I hardly paid for public transport for about three years!

Anything we wanted to do believe, we did. It was all about "getting on rowdy", we always took it in turns stealing petrol, I took it to another level by myself though, coz I got addicted to stealing petrol even though I always had money I would travel far coz I had christened so many petrol stations. As soon as they saw a car with newspaper over the number plates, it was bait!

Damien and I shared swearing, bad association, cars, drugs, stealing, and Champagne. We were on a quest to steal everything not believing in paying. We also shared our favourite negative rap music such as Flip mode squad, Busta, Wu Tang, and DMX.

The excuse with loads of the stuff I did and actions I carried out and I suppose, I tried to justify, was like, what's the point in paying? When I can get it for free. We had major selfish, self-centred mentalities, everywhere as far as we were concerned was our 'manor'.

I got to the stage. Anything I needed or wanted I stole it!!!

Damian was an attractive mixed race brother, he attracted a lot of haters and beautiful girls, that side got out of hand, and to cut the long story short Damian decided to settle down, so *he got married!* I was his best man and his wife Leone's friend was I suppose the best lady all four of us standing there at that registry office and Damian actually "tied the knot". It was deep coz anything we said we would do, we did. And Damian said he would marry his girlfriend and he did. We were doers.

We were both well known, and popular respected criminals.

Our vocabulary contained filth! The f word, b word, p word, shut up, and rowdy. *We both had a very, very well known, close friend and bodyguard he was our personal helper our bonafied. His name was Wilson.*

He was a strong wooden baseball bat! Cute guy, very loyal and strong, and never let us down!

As we got older it got to a point where I wanted to quit smoking and stop stealing and he did too, so we decided to try to help each other. We planned to get a job and start doing things properly.

I failed my theory-driving test four times and the fifth time I was five minutes late and the head guy didn't let me do it. I was so angry I spat on him and threw a chair at him and bought a new fake driver's licence. I started renting cars with hustled dirty money.

We both eventually got a job at pizza hut and both got fired, the same day, for riding the delivery bikes on the pavements at high speed, going through red lights and not delivering the pizza on time.

Then Damian got a job at a car place then he got me a job there valeting cars. As we cleaned the cars we got to drive people's exclusive and sports cars, showing them off, posing around the manor. Then Damian stole a beautiful exclusive BMW, I enjoyed posing in that car and wanted to try and sell it for him, before he got caught. I got fired from that place, coz I was not really needed anymore. Damian never returned the BMW, he took about two, three weeks off work, then later got caught by the police and was fired.

He was fortunate the company did not press charges. The next plan was to get a record deal and to break the stealing and robbing habit.

So I got some tracks done and we done a demo tape and I started to go through a phase of dying my hair different mad bright colours, and got a manager whom I later found out was trying to rip us off, Damian then lost interest.

We were gonna remain friends forever, but we started drifting away coz he was now a married man and trying to take it serious.

I had moved out to a nice plush place of my own and started making money off credit card fraud and ordering goods to my address and selling it. I had a couple of big parties, and made money from them. I loved to party and I was a good dancer and mover in those days. I invented a few of my own moves. We had so much fun on the club scene, we nearly got killed a few times. One time Damian must have got into some drama once when a gang tried to jack him for his chain so we left the club to get a gun with three of his cousins to come back and shoot them. We did come back but only one person had the gun but the dudes were nowhere to be found. Damian was like a twin brother I never had, he always helped to bail me out from the police station so my parents did not get stressed finding out and vice versa.

I remember one incident we went to the Notting Hill carnival in London, we stole some liquor before hand. I was so charged (high), I drunk so much beer and spirits and chain-smoked on drugs, I got wild I went loopy. When I arrived at the carnival. I started fighting everyone, and blatantly dipping my hand into peoples pockets, pinning people up, on a quest to rob everyone.

I got a big buzz out of grabbing people by their clothes and neck, and dragging people up. I must have got punched in the face about twice and not felt a thing by the men who fought back and ran off and must have thought I was crazy!

I persistently continued to rob and *"get on Rowdy" at the carnival.*

Then the police started to notice what Damian and I were doing so they stopped us, me especially coz I had lost it, they warned me and left.

When I got to Burger King in Park Royal, London, I literally, smashed up the whole place and knocked the tables, tills, and chairs all over the place. Coz the manager was rude and took long to serve me. I remember him screaming and locking himself in the manager's room. So I took my anger out on the restaurant. Until my knuckles swelled up and I felt pain, then I walked to the club, out of my head (uncontrollably drunk & high).

Within five minutes of being in the club I got arrested, it was so obvious it was me they were looking for 'A black guy with bright blonde hair'.

I was the worst, I was always the worst one, the fire starter, the worst thief, and the eager and excited one, but it was Damien that landed in jail!

"One Extreme To The Next"

It's funny coz when Damian went inside, after months and moths later it seemed like I was on my own, in my own little world. I then diverted to *church*. On a mission to find peace and God! This is how it happened.

One night I was out with my friends, Eddie, Sachel and Ryan, and I must have started beating up a Pizza Hut delivery driver near by and revved his motorbike engine coz I wanted the Pizza he was delivering, but he did not want to give it to me.

So I was just making trouble unnecessarily, "I was on rowdy mode ", silly, I got the pizza in the end, coz he ran off. Instead of eating it, I just threw it like a mad man? Eddie was not going to take me to the BBQ anymore and started shaking his head saying he weren't taking me to his friend's Jenny's BBQ, but I insisted and insisted I was calming down! Somehow we made our way to the BBQ, and I met Curtis, Million, Jenny, Charlotte and Tope at Jenny's BBQ. I was so drunk that night and it was as if these guys disabled my drunkenness, by truly ministering to me with love.

I believe now there was strong positive vibes, peace and joy that it over powered my drunken state! I could relate to Curtis, I felt he was real, maybe coz he had a gold teeth as well and he seemed my age and seem to have been where I had been, and we just clicked straight away! I went clubbing that night after the BBQ and agreed to follow Curtis to church the next day. The thing is, I have always been a man of my word, and so if I say I would do something, I always would.

I came back from clubbing about [7.30a.m] and heard a beep outside my window about [10.15a.m], I looked out the window tired, and to my surprise I saw Curtis, I thought is he for real?

115

So I jumped in the toilet washed my teeth and jumped into his car with the same clothes I clubbed with, which smelt of smoke and I went to church.

I had a hard, hang over, and when I got to the church I was sleepy throughout the whole service but the place seemed cool, there were loads of beautiful ladies there, and loads of youth it seemed to be kosher so I just relaxed. Then near the end this Pastor called Brian Houston, from a church called Hill song in Australia, gave an alter call, asking people who wanted to give their lives to Christ and get salvation or re dedicate their lives back to God, should come forward.

He said: "there are many of you in here today who want to be made whole", right there and then the Holy Spirit was knocking on the door to my heart, I felt this man of God was talking to me and I wanted to be made whole! What did I have to lose?

I had tried everything in search for a peace and lived my life to the max. All the money I made, the girls I slept with, the cars, gold, drugs, alcohol, partying was not enough it was temporary peace and joy. I suddenly remembered reading in the Bible once "In God is fullness of joy", that's what I needed forever the fullness of that joy. I started to have a strong pull "right there" the Spirit was drawing me, my heart was beating faster, but I was trying to avoid it suddenly my foot just walked, not me? "It come like" someone was using a remote control, to direct me forward. I was like what am I doing? There I was being set free for good! I closed my eyes cried and said the salvation prayer and got hold of God again!

What if Eddie hadn't taken me or avoided going to the BBQ?

What if? I don't think I would be writing this book?

I stole five brand new white leather bound Bibles the following week that I went to church, at a near by well known book store. I must have stolen over ten bibles from that place. I was so zealous, being a new Christian and being made whole that, I was on a mini fire for God.

It wasn't right stealing Bibles but at the time I just wanted to spread the good news and explain the peace I felt to other people. I gave one of those bibles to my brother and mother. I then tried to associate with new Christian friends, and disassociate with criminal friends round me, but there was always a "strong hold" an offer a wheeling and a dealing going on, a last move, it got intense with God especially when I nearly died again.

I had been to court more than twenty times, now! Plus twice on my birthday! My probation officer couldn't help me, I couldn't open up to nobody or relate with anyone positive!

I was fighting to keep my zeal and focus!

I wanted to live right; I just desired to be right! Man it was hard!

My Life "Was" This Cycle Below!

Age: 7 yrs saw ghost, was abused and exposed to sex, stealing.

Age: 15 yrs arrested for the first time, stealing.

Age: 16 yrs bad grades B in drama though! I was told if I didn't get to the exam late, I would have got grade A.

Got fired from burger king. Stealing. A Thief.

Age: 17 yrs fraud fake money, criminal.

Age: 18 yrs stopped going church with my parents. Ended up in court and convicted of driving whilst disqualified, banned from driving. On probation for two years. Criminal.

Age: 19yrs kicked out of college, court case, band from Ealing area, stopped going to church all together. Did nude modelling, Bank fraud £9,450.60 found the bank statement. Community service. Criminal

Age: 20 yrs robbed a woman and man, court case assault, got caught doing fraud with benefit cheques. Actor. Criminal.

Age: 21 yrs got girlfriend pregnant, lived by myself. Court case on my birthday nearly landed in jail! Actor. Found God again!

Age: 22 yrs I was growing in the things of God, I had my first Christian girlfriend, and then we broke up! I masturbated; I was battling with lust! I ain't got nothing to hide! I'm set free!

Age: 23 yrs I was an usher, counsellor, and evangelist at the church I attended!

Age: 24 yrs I was hurt and went through great depression! Overcame great depression! Started preaching. And now hitting hard with the Word of God, daily defeating the devil!

"Seen..........................

It got so dyer with the police, they were aware of me and a lot of them liked to harass me. "Okay maybe I was out of order a couple of times, but they liked to bother me man".

(The Feds) arrested me one night, one time, for being drunk and disorderly coz I was attacking people. But the feds ended up taking me to the hospital coz I collapsed in the police station. It seemed like a big dream and a fat blackout! I must have woken up on a bed the next morning with a needle in my left arm attached to a drip machine thing, that hospital bed felt weird! I got up and all I could taste was coniac, and I stunk of vomit and alcohol, it was sprayed all over my shirt.

The nurse said: the police got scared when I "threw up"(vomit) at the police station on the floor and collapsed!

I had woken up in hospital in Essex London with fatal alcohol poisoning, on coniac that I drank the night before. The nurse said I was lucky I could have died! It was not luck though! It was *GRACE,* big fat *GRACE* the *GRACE* from God! I must have drunk just more than half a bottle of coniac. 40% volume!!! Some one once told me that was, like drinking half a pint of petrol?

When Damian came out of jail, I had now found church. I was trying to settle in, and I had truly found God at this stage of my life and held on to Him! I had even given up smoking at this stage!

I had my slight girl issues, I had got one pregnant and thought a particular one had my baby, without telling me, but I couldn't prove it!

I was like Nah, the devil ain't gonna steal my joy, my focus is to be right in the sight of God. I can do it, so in time I got involved in church and that's what truly built character in me to take me to the next level in Christ Jesus. I became an usher at the church and did Psalms chapter 91 verse 1 & chapter 92 verse 13-14 the rest is history.

I Wrote On Paper: Commitments with God and stuck it on my wall:

1999 Keep out of trouble!

1 no more raving or (partying unless it's with close friends)

2. No more Blazing (smoking drugs)

3. No more drinking

4. No more lashing (stealing)

5. No more playing (sleeping around having sex)

6. No more lashing

7. No more swearing

8. No more backstreet dealing or buying dodgy stuff

9. Start regular tithing and offering

10. Be prayerful

11. Pray for other people more than myself

12. Read my bible & scriptures

13. Honour your elders & parents & women

Anything that was a problem or a habit I always identified with, I wrote down on paper!

It took me three years to overcome and carry those written things out! Three years to manifest and the result is: *I conquered my written commitments with God! And I'm now set free!*

I (Habakkuk Two, Twoed it!) **I realise I still have a lot of cleaning out to go and I will never be perfect till I get to heaven!**

I never had counselling or could speak to any one about my problems "I sure needed it though! Believe! But I found it hard to open up to anyone, including, Pastors, Probation officers, Solicitors, Parents or Friends. In the quest of being a righteous man!

In 2001 Damian became a father of a beautiful baby girl called Kalesha and asked me to be Godfather. He was going to take care of his responsibility and he cared, but needed a breakthrough! I advised him and told him a lot of things he could use to his advantage, I wanted to do all in my power to help him and I tried!

I tried to pull him to church but Damian weren't feeling it. However he did manage to give his life to God, but went to jail again coz he stuck with the wrong crowd and association!

I fortunately managed to take Damian to a church once, it was a church concert where he gave his life from his heart to Jesus Christ!

2002 I lost Damian, my best friend, a dear friend, he died before he turned 24. My pain began! I cried for weeks. The greatest depression of my life hit me!

As I carried his coffin that day, everything in me cried, I walked in the reality I did not want to believe! I know he is in a better place! Heaven!

In 2002 in the middle of the tragedy and all the depression I was faced with, the church I attended and pastor I put my trust and all in, failed me!

The pastor was messing with women, emotions, peoples lives, money, and battling with lust, pornography, pride and greed! It all just suddenly came out in the open! Just when I was enjoying my relationship with God, being a Christian and living a right life! Delivered and set free from, sleeping around, masturbation, stealing, and anger!

It suddenly felt like my world crumbled, everything just came to a stand still! Bitterness, anger, frustration, depression! Kicked in! BIG TIME!

I could not comprehend that this church I attended was falling down, on top of that I was labelled the black sheep of the church? Could you believe I was banned from coming in to the church, that church I attended, that church that was like my second home. I suppose in the natural I deserved it coz after all I did attack the pastor!

I will never forget that day the pastor called a meeting for church 'members only' to supposedly repent and confess to the church members about what he had done. Lo and behold he was still acting all puffed up and would not step down from his position as a pastor and confess about what he had done. It seemed everyone was under a trance and was worshiping this pastor and everybody seemed fine with this man's actions and it seemed like everyone was just willing to forget the damaged lives.

This meant to be man of God had caused major destruction, on top of that he had hired security guards, some of whom I recognised from night clubs I used to club in before I was saved (Christian).

I felt this was a big insult to God, God's house and to the congregation. This made me more angry and I personally felt that I could not see that this pastor had a contrite heart, or an ounce of faith if he felt he needed to hire five huge security guards. He should have taken his consequences like a man!

Lots of things were going through my mind I felt betrayed, I was deeply hurt that my friends were abused and that the ladies that I looked upon as my sisters were violated, people were queuing up in a line to shake this pastor's hand without knowing what he was repenting for or what he had done, this 'pastor' s repent service' turned into 'man' 'worship'.

I made a drastic decision to queue up and beat the pastor up! So I got in line twisted my rings on my fingers round and when I saw the pastor face to face instead of shaking his hand I looked him in the eye and grabbed his neck with my left arm then the pastor screamed for his life, I guess he saw the pain and anger in my eyes, then I swung a mean punch with my right arm to his face and kicked out at him then I was suddenly pulled from behind by two security guards, what a disgrace all this was happening in a church!

The security nearly strangled me to death on the floor I was lifted by my neck by four security guards and I was on my last breath could you believe I nearly died!!!

I was then used as a battering ram head first carried and thrown out of the church by the five security guards then briefly rushed by these hired security guards who were twice my size.

A well-known white senior pastor from Rhema ministries South Africa who I thought was a big coward for not standing up to the pastor that let us down, was standing there in the front on stage, just gazing at what was happening and not saying nothing. He was also meant to be the spiritual father (mentor) of the pastor. It now makes sense that it was just a cover up.

The pastor and leader of the church I attended was meant to be accountable to him but he wasn't, he made it clear he was not accountable to nobody.

Anyways the well-known white pastor from Rhema ministries South Africa came up to me outside as the security guards left me, and wanted to pray with me. I told him to 'F' off in rage and anger, he looked at me in shock then he cussed back at me in shock!

I was in no position to calm down or let any pastor touch me or speak into my life as I realised and got a revelation at this stage that pastor or no pastor it is a title and a pastor is just a 'man'.

The actions I took against the pastor that let me down, was a result of anger, but I understand now that it did not justify my actions, although the Pastor called me up that week and apologised to me for what had happened to me but not to anyone else which I felt meant he considered me a threat!

At this point in my Christian walk I lost trust for pastors and leadership, I wanted to destroy, and take matters into my own hands, it got to a point where I started looking at a gun magazine and even made calls and hung up, I nearly called a old friend who could get me hit men for cheap! Coz I wanted to kill people! But eventually realised that the battle was not mine, it was the Lord's! It was spiritual, the devil tried to invade my mind and use my evil feelings! To his benefit but I snapped out of it!

I'll never forget 2002 coz I had a nervous break down!

God, I felt like doing so much crazy things! And wanted to go wild and back to "rowdy time". I tried to take my pain to God many times, but it was so painful and difficult. I just didn't want to talk to God at the time, I supposed I almost lost faith, coz I had got so deep in it! And it seemed to have failed me! But it was a test! A big one! The biggest test I ever faced in my life!

I now realise though! The bigger the test, the higher the calling! The stronger I would be, but only one person wanted for me not to pass that test! "You guessed it Satan".

With this situation I was faced with at the time, I was so weak, that I had allowed bitterness, hate, depression and anger to take over my life and choke my soul. I stopped eating for months, I lost weight, I lost confidence in man and I lost my joy and lost my peace.

I was in such a bad way for a solid 1 year, I struggled to face the next day, I had suicidal thoughts, I had lost the will to live or live right anymore,

I actually thought I was going mad, I did bizarre things as I drove my car, like over speeding, not stopping at red lights and almost knocking people over.

One day as I was driving my car I just stopped my car in the middle of the road and cried for 10 minutes, about Damian, about the church, about my life, about the pastor that messed up, about everything. Cars were driving past beeping the horn at me as I was holding up traffic. After about 20 minutes I put my car in gear and carried out a U turn then I head straight for the Doctors Surgery. I had made up my mind that I was going to take the easy, quick and wrong way out and admit myself into hospital and go on anti-depressants, or tranquillisers to take the pain I felt away.

When I got to the Doctors Surgery I started screaming saying: "I want to see the doctor now", I said the same thing about three times until the doctor heard me coz I was so loud, he came out of his office and told me to stop screaming, and firmly told me he was not going to see me and told me to go home or he would call the police. I looked at him with shock and silence then ran out of the Doctors Surgery and jumped into my car and drove home, when I got home I took out my anger on my family, when my mother or father asked if I was okay I switched, by screaming like a mad then walking away.

I was so moody, I wouldn't open up to anyone, coz I isolated myself so much for a whole year it had heartened my heart.

My mind was being attacked severely, I wanted to destroy and fuel my anger out, It felt like my oppression and depression was going to last forever but it was for only a season. Now looking back I realised I had lost all sense of patience. I tried to fit back in the world, such as clubbing, smoking, cussing, fighting taking out my anger on anyone that slightly ticked me off but that did not work, I found I could not fit back into this lifestyle that I left behind a long time ago, plus the righteous way felt much better, deep down in my Spirit I knew it.

I finally took authority one day and took my pain to God, I could not pray for months, but when I tried little by little I got back my zeal! My prayer for moths was: "God help me", "God give me strength", "God restore me" if I did not say all of these it was one of these prayers, which in time open the way for God to start restoring me and ordering my steps again. Which meant I had to be prepared to be hurt again, trust again and submit to leadership again.

The devil himself did not want me to past the test but I did pass!

Something I couldn't do by myself, but by letting the Holy Spirit God Almighty do, by believing and trusting God!

I made a choice to reach out and pick up my healing!

When I cried to God, I released all my burdens to God by prayer and songs of worship then a season later I was in a position to really forgive and fulfil my purpose!

I eventually came to realise, again, nobody is perfect and we all make mistakes. Just coz my sin ain't out in the open what right have I got to judge all pastors, leaders or anyone?

Although my philosophy at the time was, if it were Moses that did what he did as a leader he would have got stoned to death, but the fact of the matter is we are all sinners and we are living by pure grace!

And we have "ALL FALLEN SHORT"!!!!!!!!!!!!!!!

I had to go through a long process of healing and I believe I am healed now by faith!

Chapter 14

Searching For Fame

I was about 18-19 years old now, and was searching for fame. Damian was in jail then. And I did not want a regular job, since my past experiences with work. I always wanted to work in a job I enjoyed doing! So I decided to pursue my dream as an actor!

When I found some soberness I followed my dream of acting and started to follow it through, I supposed I was going through a phase of trying to fit in as someone different and unique as an entertainer. I went through dying my hair different colours, and having different mad hairstyles. I was still a criminal trying to find my destiny, but then again, I have always felt I knew what I wanted!

My first journey into fame began when I came out of a club in Piccadilly Circus London, I was always in style in those days. I had all the latest and unique designer clothes in those days. I loved fashion. I liked the Armani, YSL, Gucci and my favourite at the time was Moschino, I had style. I loved it man.

That night I had spent all my money on champagne and drinks, I was so drunk and had nothing left to get home, so I started knocking on car windows at the traffic lights.

And doing some nutty stuff like standing in front of cars to stop and demand money. So much cars were beeping their horn at me to get out of the way, I was causing mini catastrophe on the roads in central London.

It was about 5-6A.M in the morning, cars were driving and swerving past me. Then suddenly a white guy in a posh Toyota jeep stopped and wound down his electric window, he asked: "what do you want? I said some money to get home, he then said he liked my gold teeth and asked: how much do you want? I told him. And he gladly gave it to me.

As he gave me the money he passed me a gold coloured business card and then said: "get a job".

Then drove off. The next day, when I was sober, I was chuffed to read the business card had written on it: **Models one exclusive male models and escorts**, I called the number on the business card in excitement. I thought this was my break into fame!

"Anyways" I met the guy that handed me the business card on Monday in Camden London, he picked me up in his car and we went to a posh studio flat where I started underwear modelling. The guy convinced me that he would get me modelling work for top fashion designers such as Calvin Klein and Versace, and various other top designer underwear brands and companies.

I found myself compromising, bit by bit and I ended up doing nude modelling, for dirty pornographic magazines, supposedly for Holland and Germany, and then been pressured, deviously with more cash, into being a male escort, thank God I did not do it.

I was offered a lot of money, but was put off at the fact I would go out on dates with anyone, meaning old, young, homosexuals, heterosexuals, male or female and may have to have sex with them! I was only nineteen and I felt I might catch some disease so I was put off that. As time went by I was offered more money and did more and more explicit nude shots and poses!

One day the man taking the pictures started to ask me if I had ever done or considered doing a pornographic film. I said I might consider it, coz I was tempted by the amount of money he was offering.

Suddenly the guy put an explicit sexual video on and told me to watch it, it had the women and men I was going to be filming with, if I agreed to it.

I remember this day very clearly coz it was a day I'll never forget, I was watching the video then paused the pornographic film, I then went to the toilet, came back unpaused the film, and I heard shuffling behind me, when I turned round to my disgust and shock I saw the guy masturbating!

I was so shocked, I didn't know whether to kick the man, spit, shout I was thinking in my mind, is this really happening? Then he asked me if I would rub baby oil on his chest, I found myself squirting baby oil on his chest then walking back to my seat in confusion and shock, on what I just did, I look back on this now and think I did not know what the hell I was doing?

I feel now I done this coz I was money hungry and naïve, I wanted to break into fame so bad, that I was nearly prepared to do what it took. I feel another reason why I was in this predicament was coz I relied on the money too, so I wanted to make sure I got paid that night.

Anyways continuing with what happened that night. I continued to watch the film, and when the guy finished what he was doing, he went to the toilet and came back then offered me a drink I was fuming! I said: *"No I don't want a drink"*, with an attitude, I thought what a nerve this guy had to ask me such a question after using his hands to touch his penis, I then said I didn't want to take anymore pictures for the day. He offered me even more money for some reason, which I took, but I didn't even do anything?

He always dropped me home, but today as he was dropping me off, I felt very, very, very uncomfortable, he kept asking me if there was anything I wanted or wanted to do, or if I liked prostitutes. I was tempted, but I just insisted to be dropped off home.

We started to talk about the film that he wanted me to do and I had come to a instant decision and told him I didn't want to do it any more but knew who would like to do it, and even more models he could use, coz I told some of my friends that I did nude modelling and they wanted to give it a try especially coz of the volume of money I got just for two hours work.

When I declined the pornographic film I thought there's my chance to be on television gone, but then again I didn't want to start my career with pornography on my portfolio! I thought I could catch something and was aware of Aids and the possibility of putting myself in the position of catching that nasty virus!

When we got outside my house, the guy exposed himself to me some more! This guy was a white wealthy guy between his late thirties and early forties who was also an accountant. *You would have thought this guy had his head and career screwed on!*

That was obviously not the case!

He then said to me in the car, he liked me, and found me attractive, and would like to have a relationship with me, he asked me to come and live in his house and I wouldn't have to do anything, just be there with him.

He offered me money and my own place. I was even more shocked and disgusted I thought what the hell is this? The amount of things I wanted to say, I somehow held in coz I thought about the money he'd given me for the night and I said in shock and tension "No" I don't feel that way.

I just want to model for top designers, and get on television. He then said he respected that but if I changed my mind to contact him.

I thought this was sick, when I walked into my house I was dazed. I have always thought and said if a batty man, homosexual chat me up I would punch him up, and spit on him.

I was disgusted at the fact I ever socialised with this guy and he conned me into thinking he was just my friend and my agent." *What a bump"!*

The Price of Fame

What if I said yes to living with him?

Or done the escorting job?

Or done the porn film?

Coz I loved money and wanted a house and car and the rest of it.

What if I did?

I probably would have been twisted by now, or a bisexual, or a drug addict to escape reality of the shame! I never met this guy again after that but when I wanted some bulk cash I thought about a quick escorting job or nude modelling job, so I called him coz the money was good.

I wanted those pounds, nothing but currency was on my mind, but I always got an answering machine and left a message. When he would reply he took every opportunity to chat me up and ask me to come to his house in Brent Cross, London, I soon got the message and started to feel like I was acting desperate. I just cut him off and threw away the business card.

I found it hard to do it at first, coz I made loads of money from that nude modelling thing, but one thing was leading to another.

What if I went down the wrong road? My life would have change like I'm sure many people's life has that took such wrong path!

What if?

Please read <u>1Timothy chapter 6 verse 10</u>

Please read <u>1 John chapter 2 verse 16-17</u>

I had to duck out, and bounce!

Your Identity Is Important!

I found an agent later that year and she got me my first role on television "The Bill" as a criminal "What a coincidence aye", and a Converse advert. Then I landed a few other auditions, commercials and television productions later.

I finally got my break! But not the big break! I did various drama productions and got my first series, I always went to the after parties and screenings, mixing with few celebrities but again there were homosexuals who tried to chat me up.

I was not having it, but could not express disapproval of them openly in the so-called entertainment scene, coz they were more than accepted, respected and liked.

As far as a lot of people were concerned it was normal to be gay? I would always get drunk I would sometimes compromise by flirting with men or women and find men's arms around my shoulders but would realise and walk off laughing, then chat up the ladies.

I started to find most of the people in control of the films and media were in fact homosexual, I just started to get irritated and wanted a *"BREAK"* I wanted to be a full-time actor not a struggling one. The more things I did the more homosexuals I saw, I did not want to accept them as they were, or agree with their ways, so in a way I was heading down a dead end road, coz the majority of people in the industry controlling stuff i.e. writers and directors were gay!

It was getting to the point that if I was not friends with gay people or accepted what they did and mingle I weren't going anywhere.

I started getting impatient and angry!

I was about 21 now and I was fighting to be a good Christian at the time too. Weighing up my belief and career was hard! *"Trust"*, I also started to live by myself at this time, and got by, by fraud, working at a well known supermarket three times a week, purposely, to get credit card numbers, I was obsessed with swords, I must have ordered five swords, six BB guns, three daggers, a bow and arrow archery set I'm glad the credit card number bounced back coz if it didn't I wonder what shenanigans I would have got up to with these weapons? I didn't have to work, so when I felt lazy I ordered more goods with people's credit card numbers to my address, such as mobile phones mainly and other stuff then sold them.

The entertainment field was such a challenge, spiritually, mentally, and sexually. I was also having battles coz I thought I was going to jail, I was addicted to weed (drugs), alcohol and sex!

All this was made abundantly available in the new lifestyle I was living as an aspiring actor!

Scenario: one of the dangers, being an actor. When I went to Czech republic, I went wild, I was some loose cannon up there, and it was fun! Getting the opportunity to do an advert abroad. I got this job as a result of an audition. "Man at auditions you have to impress the casting directors otherwise you ain't getting anything Believe".

I could back flip, so I pulled it off at this particular audition and got the part, as a result I got given spending money, flight, hotel, and taxi all-inclusive, on top of that I got a fat cheque. I nearly collapsed out there, coz I smoked my brains out! And got drunk at clubs out there.

The clubs were so explicit out there, there were young men and women having sex blatantly in the lounge area, all you had to do was go to find a seat and there it was, "pure sin going on!

I am so ashamed of this, but I forced myself onto one of the girls from London that night, as I followed her into her hotel room, lust came upon me and dominated my body and mind plus I was beyond drunk, she started to massage me in her room and she told me she had a boyfriend but as far as I was concerned then, *I wanted to get my freak on, so "I got on rowdy!*

As an actor I still stole, I can't believe I started stealing at the airport when I was in Germany. I sometimes think I did some silly things that could have got me into a stupid predicament! But why did I do it? It was the norm to me, I didn't care and felt it was easy! (But it was a problem)

One day I made a difficult decision about my life and lifestyle I was living as an actor!

All the auditions I had attended, all the parts I appeared in, music videos, promotional work, drama, films, commercials, all the contacts I built and gathered, all the artistes I met, all the future productions, films, commercial, modelling I could take part in. upon all I ever did. It was time to count the costs. I knew there were big hindrances, demons, immorality, temptations and challenges the entertainment field carried, and it was getting challenging, coz of the industry and association it brought.

So I decided if I'm not going to get parts that edify, this industry/ministry is not for me!

I guess my desire for being an actor has not completely dissolved, if I get the opportunity to do something I feel is satisfactory and beneficial I probably will.

DON'T LOOSE YOUR IDENTITY: "find yourself, know who you are and L-i- v- e   r- i –g- h- t!

I am no longer a thief, and no longer an angry person, and I wouldn't say I am no longer an actor but acting is a skill to me, but not something I pursue.

I still have gold teeth, gold rings, wear designer clothes, but have a different heart, I no longer sleep around, smoke, steal, fight, get angry (all the time), switch, swear (cuss) has popped out a few times but out of *100%* about *5%*. My life is simpler and I have the chance and peace to think about how to change things for good!

"Don't ever let anybody tell you you're not someone, coz you're not a star, celebrity, a doctor or any of that jazz! You need to tell yourself:

'I am someone!'

God has made you great, unique, more than a conqueror!

So 'DIVINE PURPOSE LIVES INSIDE OF YOU'.

'I ain't trying to put you off fame', or your dreams but I am making you aware of what to expect and what type of industry your getting into!

Catch Tha Revelation...........

Preach
Preacher

Preach Preacher

Chapter 15

Habits And Basics

Habits are easy to get into and hard to break off, I remember when I was in a comfort zone in my early Christian walk coz I was new to the Christ life, and been somewhere, where I thought I had it all.

I figured God was just a friend I'll call on sometimes for back up. At the time I felt I didn't need Him all the time.

I had the cars, the house, the clothes, the drugs, girls, sex, the scash money, I was living it up, so I thought, did I have peace though? *'Nope'*, I had enemies, people who were jealous of me people who wanted to know what I did. I was in and out of court every month, often arrested, finding myself in the police station cell many times, stripped searched many times.

Anger ruled me, I had been beaten up so many times, I had beat people up many times but all this was not really even major to me, it was waking up knowing there was a God but not enjoying His benefits!! This is the truth. I had no peace, no focus and no integrity.

I have experienced many things in life, one of the things I will never forget is when I had a strong out of body experience, this happened when I fell from a first floor balcony and became unconscious.

I remember drowning and being on my last breath proceeding to sink, another experience I had was being physically attacked whilst sleeping and trying to sleep which has happened many times.

I nearly got killed several other times.

This entire saga I went through just proves to you that God has totally changed my life and has taken me out of my mess and had mercy and grace on a wretch like me!

I believe in miracles, in angels, the Holy Spirit, spiritual warfare, heaven, hell, healing, the blessings and the benefits I have found about God's wisdom.

"You know something it's phenomenal the way we can breathe, walk, sleep and wake up. Living life.

"Well if you don't think so I personally think it is.

"Okay let me not go off the rails.

As I've been sharing my life with you, my struggles, temptations and so on and so forth. We all have had problems, issues and situations that seem like it was gonna take forever to resolve. Little do we know we need to go through them to become stronger!

Have you checked out what **Galatians chapter 5 verse 22** says my brother my sister, it talks about the fruit of the spirit and **Ecclesiastes chapter 3 verse 1** talks about a time for everything yes **"EVERYTING"**

"Hey I'm not perfect, no one is perfect I am still learning a lot of things about God and about life even now, even down to the way I speak I still have a few loose slang I am trying to get rid of. I feel it's good to talk properly and people know what you're talking about and knowing how to express yourself. It all takes time.

The bottom line is God will use you as you are. Meaning He will meet you where you're at when you decide to become a Christian!

I am not well spoken, although I used to speak properly but due to association and the environment I grew up in, my words got polluted by slang and so called street lingo.

I would also like to still sort out things like my maths, my memory, I forget things easy and that never used to be the case but blazing that skunk weed (marijuana, ganja, drugs) messed up my memory a bit and brought out more of the badness in me.

I wanna fix my time I spend with God, be more patient and lots of other things I am struggling with, but you know what, my heart is willing and ready and I will forever aim to be like Jesus and love like He did.

When you're in Christ you are a new creature. Saved by grace, in Christ all things are possible! Amen.

I have really desired to be right and go straight but did not think for one moment that I would be totally saved and walk right for God.

When I mean walk right I mean certain areas, which a lot of 'so called Christians' don't even do. Even I didn't use to do it, the 'Christianity basics' such as not swearing, sleeping around, stealing, getting drunk, raving it up in every club in town, blazing (smoking drugs), fighting, forgiving the list goes on.

I personally used to think it was okay to do these things if you just respect God and pray, I thought it was fine, that was my frame of mind before. As I got to know G-O-D I found out it was not so, I can't possibly fear God if I thought that was okay. It's funny coz I thought those things were okay until *January, February 2000* when I woke up, I saw the light and smelt the coffee!

My God I lived a lot of my fantasies!

I had a friend that always said these things are not really bad, he justified it by saying that this is the times we live in, everyone does it and he said, God said if you only *'believe'* it's fine? So in other words he was saying it was fine to sleep around, steal, stump on people's faces, get drunk, and get high.

That word that was sown into my life added more blindness. Other people would say foolishness like just give thanks to God and that's it.

The fact of the matter is you can't just *'believe'.* When you *'believe'* something has got to change!

One day I really, really, really, thought long and hard about this issue and I came to a conclusion that, not everyone is doing these bad things or caught up in this messy predicament I was in, I was choosing to be?

It would have helped if I read the Word ('The Holy Bible'= God's Mind) and started to apply it, but I didn't coz I was anorexic of the Word ('The Holy Bible'= God's Mind) so I got weak again and fell into my old routine.

It was Just *"yes"* again to sin and compromising. Being drunk at least three times a week, high on drugs nearly every day which didn't help the situations, plus when people in general and Christians used to say why did I still go clubbing and raving and drink champagne and listen to all these filthy music then come to church the following day? I wouldn't listen I would say to myself what the hell is wrong with a little fun? This is the real world, but then again that was causing my downfall.

I was promoting I was a Christian to people and trying to tell people about Jesus, telling them to come church, in fact the odd few people came, the other lot would call me an hypocrite.

Scenario 1: I would tell a girl how good God and church is and the next weekend I was flirting with one of her friends or be slow wining and grinding dancing in a club with another girl?

Scenario 2: I would tell certain friends come to church and they would say I am smoking weed and robbed someone the other day, and done this and that and I am telling them they are wrong and they need to come to church and praise God? What kind of example am I?

On top of that talking with big fat combinations of cuss words attached? Is that how Christians are?

It was so painful at times trying to tell people about God and knowing in the back of my mind I'm doing worse things than them and then offering to bring them to church in my rented car, rented with dirty money.

In a way though I thought I was right but I wasn't I was a capital big WRONG, but then again that is the way I used to think.

When you turn Christian and you're not as upright as you should be, coz God is God and because you have accepted Him and have made that special supernatural transaction with Him allowing Him to release the 'Holy Spirit' in you to contact and communicate with Him, He always shows you stuff and gives you endless visions, coz the Holy Spirit directs our steps and brings conviction!

That's what the Holy Spirit does once He is in you, He convicts you, reveals truth, and the truth hurts, but truth always *'SETS YOU FREE'* but one likes to avoid it at times. Coz the sin is sweet and life seems easy.

One day I caught the biggest revelation and that scripture in the Bible (God's Mind) *'your body is a temple'* *"heavy revy"* hit me, this scripture jumped out and 'bear hugged' me **1 Corinthians Chapter 3 verse 16** and then this one **1 Corinthians Chapter 6 verse 19** *"bang, bang, double portion, these scriptures came alive to me, and became a revelation and reality! Although I had seen it before it didn't mean jack to me those other times, but this time a certain Pastor emphasised on it and bwoooooooooy did I feel a big, big conviction, those words of truth, positive vibes and encouragement"* were sown and I stopped drinking and smoking instantly. It lasted about a week and a half, then I was being offered it in parties, clubs, friends houses and my flesh accepted straight away.

Always excuses, excuses, excuses, but also again the *'force and power'* of the company I kept, and places I went to had a major impact and influence on my actions.

'BAD COMPANY CORRUPT GOOD MORALS'.

Everytime I would think no I shouldn't blaze (smoke drugs), then automatically seconds later I just found myself doing it telling myself it's just a social thing and a one off.

"YEAH RIGHT CAUGHT UP SON" automatic thoughts would come into my head and saturate my mind with why I should do it. The enemy would influence my thoughts and say: *"okay I don't feel happy right now, it will comfort me, make me feel better, make me relaxed, feel stronger,* but really and truly all I got was a night's buzz, clothes smelling of smoke, a sore throat in the morning and red eyes.

As time went by I hated the drugs and myself, the Holy Spirit that was activated kept convicting me too, coz I was grieving my Spirit!

I found this habit and addiction to smoking weed was wearing me down and I realised that this drug wasn't my comforter anymore Jesus Christ was!

I would then speak to God and ask God for forgiveness, as soon as I were sober snapping out of my high state, remembering what God's Word said, and what the Pastor also said about what God's Word said. This was persistent for about a year since I made up my mind to be a real Christian and quit smoking, crime and sleeping around.

Trying to conquer all these bad habits, the guilt and fear of God, got to the point where it was chewing me up inside.

It got too much and I had got so desperate to be a proper Christian but more temptations of scandalous things were just flying at me from the left and the right, up and down, front and back, at this stage I just had to write everything I hated down on paper. All the sins I wanted to give up, I highlighted the sins one by one and stuck it on my wall so I could see it everytime I woke up.

And **ONE DAY** miraculously I just woke up and I told myself I would never smoke again, besides it made my clothes and breath smell.

From that day that desire left it was no more, one down few to go.

It was a gradual process the same with all the other habits I wanted and needed to drop instantly, I wanted to conquer these things because I just knew that I knew God was real and I was itching to show God I wanted to be used to the maximum potential.

The **Habakkuk Chapter 2 Verse 2 effect** in the Bible (God's Mind) worked effectively for me!

I was willing and lead by the Spirit and I had acquired power to lay down my first boundaries, no more drugs, no more sex, no more stealing, no more fraudulent acts, no more clubbing, no more raving with friends it tempts and arouses my flesh.

It took a loooooooooooooooooooong process to deal with these issues but I can testify today *March 2003* I can actually still say I have done it!

One is always kind of conscious about what their doing or about to do! We all know deep down what we are doing is right or wrong! You just go with the flow and ignore the facts! The truth!

Don't think for one second this testimony happened overnight bro! Coz it didn't, some things go away for a while then bounce back, the devil likes to play with us with these habits and temptation, but the fact of the matter is, it's not easy *"TO JUST GIVE UP HABITS"!*

The devil gets his strength and kick out of these habits. Especially if you are used to it and it does not seem wrong at all.

I can relate to giving up a 'HABIT', it is damn hard, trust me! You've gots to get hold of yourself and put yourself under manners and decide enough is enough and take it one step at a time and lean on 'The Holy Spirit' and Acknowledge Him!

Then once you have made one change and given up one thing, you will want to conquer the rest, that's how I did it, just have faith.

Take down your dirty posters and rap posters and put Godly things up and watch how your mind starts to open up and your focus will be right, you will have different interests and you will succeed in everything you do with the integrity of God. Remember lean not on your own understanding! God said that! You see the devil and his tricks he is the heavyweight trickster. His never-ending tricks will go on, but God has one more move!

God is always ahead, He is the creator and Greater is He who is in us!! *Hallelujah*.

'The devil is a player' but 'Jesus is the games master!' (The person in control, above, commander) In Christ Jesus we are more than conquerors!

I really thought it would take me until I was about twenty-five or thirty-years old till I really took God and my Christian walk serious, and give up minor habits, but boy when you get a revelation of what and who God is, your mind set picks up the pace! You start learning about the basic foundations things such as *INTEGRITY*, **CHARACTER**, *FOCUS*, and *AUTHORITY* that's when you're on your way and you're faith gets to be strong it needs that efficacy, *"you know what I mean"*.

It's all about the book called: **Hebrews** chapter 11 verse 6

Luke chapter 10 verse 19, **Proverbs** chapter 11 and **Proverbs** chapter 13 verse 20.

Now I can proudly say I have been checked out physically and spiritually meaning I have been to the hospital to get tested for any infections or disease (physically) and asked God to search me and order my steps (spiritually). If you are going to walk right take the right precautions and do the right thing! God is using me as a tool and I just keep learning and growing spiritually! **"Ya get me!**

After accomplishing the main habits and addiction I had thought if I can give that up I'm done, finished, I can carry on with just going to church and serving.

Not so brother, not so at all? I must have grieved the Holy Spirit within me bad, to my understanding now, coz when you accept God, the Holy Spirit is activated in you! When you're led by the Holy Spirit there are things called responsibilities?

Tasks such as fighting off the devil from your mind, praying, worshiping, spiritual maintenance and all that jazz!

Chapter 16

Don't Mess With A Christian!

The name Jesus is powerful we as Christians (Christ Like People) possess authority! Coz we are in Christ. Did you know we are higher than the angels, but they protect us. God loves thugs, you know. Jesus constantly mixed with ruff people to set them free and teach them righteousness. I feel this was because thugs are more real and more willing than religious minded people.

As I said earlier some people get the idea that a Christian is some fable somebody?

Broda don't mess with a Christian (Christ Like People), coz you don't know what you're dealing wid!

When you, or a person becomes a Christian, know matter where he or she is they have a glow, a peace a define difference about their appearance!

You can tell when a Christian (Christ Like People) walks into a room! *Don't make a Christian buss some prayers up in your backside!*

A Christian is not a person to be messed about with. Coz greater is He in Christians (Christ Like People) when you speak against one, or try to do evil, you are actually doing it onto God!

So be careful coz God is in every Christian (Christ Like People) if you want to be a real Christian (Christ Like People) activate what is inside of you!

Which is the anointing of God, which also brings you to a place of understanding. "*Can't touch this mode*".

When you have a revelation of who you are in Christ Jesus! You can really move mountains and walk on water!!!

Not all Christian (Christ Like People) are the same or appear to be righteous, there are many Christians at different levels spiritually, this is where people get their wires crossed and like to cuss Christians and churches! *STOP!*

We all go through stuff and one day a non-Christian could buck up with a Christian that is in a bad mood or not walking in the Spirit or may be a new Christian that gives the wrong impression!

I have been guilty of giving a bad impression not intentionally but I repent straight away, example, when I was driving past a traffic light it was my right of way and some dude decides to walk in front of my car with his two girlfriends while the light was green and coz I swerved past him he decides to kick my car.

Now I'm still dealing with patience and he was wrong but I could have chose to exercise patience.

I reversed parked on the corner and got out of my mother's car shouting threatening, to break his face, his friends started telling me sorry and to calm down, I felt foolish and calmed down and realised who I was in Christ!

Now sometimes our flesh nearly dominates us Christians, trying to bring out our old nature, that's why everything God says we need to take heed to His Words! And "*WALK IN THE SPIRIT*" it ain't easy.

This however does not give anyone an excuse to take advantage of the grace of God and go out and wilfully sin coz it could land you in a coffin, coz the wages of sin is death and when we are in sin we are vulnerable to death not by God's fault but our own fault.

The blood that was shed by Jesus Christ on the cross of Calvary was designed to bring you to a place of repentance! But just like police, are human beings, realise and recognise Christians (Christ Like People) are human beings too so don't mess with a Christian!

I remember when I was in my early Christian walk, and I was actually convinced I was ready to die and going to kill for my brother coz he crashed some drug dealer's car by accident and they started getting on *"shabby"* talking all sorts of jazz bout what they would do to my brother.

"These guys *'gate crashed'* into my brother's friend's house. There were three of them, one guy with a small gun in his pocket. All three of these foolish guys had made up their minds that they would not let anyone of us out of the house until my brother showed up!

I was getting so frustrated I was so vex coz they kept on going on about how much money they want from my brother and what they would do to him if they didn't get the money, but I wasn't having it and I was replying back and I said: "nah man" you ain't doing nothing to my brother!

It was a sticky situation coz one man had a gun and they were beating up my brother's friend in the room, and a little fool kept flashing the gun in his trousers, to intimidate us. My cousin Jackson kept saying there was no need for this and one went into the kitchen and got a kitchen knife and started to flash it around! Militantly!

I then got fed up of being held hostage in a house for three hours coz one person was standing by the door with the gun in his trousers, so I said I'll get some of the money for my brother, so they let me go and I went home put on my Avirex jacket and put two knives in my jacket, a long kitchen knife and a chopper (meat cleaver) and made my way to the cash point!

I went back to the house with the frame of mind of killing if they didn't let me back out! I got to the door and I wanted to stab all three of them somehow!

Starting with the one that had the gun first but when I got in I screwed up the money and threw it, they counted it and left.

I've always had that mentality, I used to say I would kill for brother or family. I would however change that mentality now to, I would die for my family!

Tha devil better back off coz I'm shining for Jesus!

The act of the flesh is dangerous, I believe when you're slipping into the flesh, and we act in the flesh, our carnal mind takes over. We are caught off guard, which can cause us to grieve the Holy Spirit.

"I'm Just Sending The Devil A Reminder For Record, You Don't Have A Clue Who You're Dealing With! Don't mess with a Christian! Do you have any idea the power and authority a Christian person possesses?

The power ain't from us it's from God, THE G-O-D,

God knows every individual, how? He knows our spirit and what He has called us to be! In-fact that is a revelation, he does actually know every individual and spirit *'being'*, He knows the flesh, that it is born with sin and that we will have a sinful nature.

How? Coz we all descend from Adam whether you believe it or not. He knows our spirit coz it is His. He has given us authority proof in tha Word (The Bible) remember the Word (The Bible) is the mind of God!

Romans chapter 8 verse 27-30: Tells us we are born for the purposed to be conformed to the image of CHRIST. That is to be Christ like. To be righteous in all Jesus Christ's ways, having the same mind set.

Samuel chapter 16 verse 7: God looks at the heart

Luke chapter 10 verse 19: God has given us authority

Acts chapter 1 verse 8: You shall receive power.

The Word of God is Deep!

Chapter 17

Character & Integrity

I used have a love hate relationship with my dad, check it now I have a good relationship with my dad now! *What change that? God or me?*

God my friend! God has done great things in my life you know.

I have never liked fake people, *sorry man, just being honest I'm still dealing with it,* people, I have always had the gift of discernment to tell if some is being real or fake, it is good to just be yourself!

I had come to a big revelation and had to accept that *"everybody is different",* we all have different characters, moods, looks, behaviours, fingerprints and all that jazz.

Don't keep getting sucked into what society says, analyse your life and things in general, there are lots of distractions in the world today that deceive, such as music videos, half naked men, and women with no integrity! You can do the music video thing, sing, and rap but the right way! By being positive and not affecting the new generation! Put all beef aside and unite, unity is the key and love: "are you feeling stirred up?

Do I have doubts? Sometimes. Do I get angry? Sometimes. Do I feel like breaking people's faces? Sometimes, do I feel like acting unrighteous? Sometimes.

Read about the character of the FLESH: **Romans chapter 7 verse 15 – 25:** when I want to do Good Evil is waiting at the door to stop me. But the last **verse 25** of **Romans chapter 7:** I thank God through Jesus Christ that I can choose to serve the law of God (Good/righteous) and not the law of the flesh (evil/unrighteous).

Things play on my mind a lot when I'm not in the Word (The Bible) and I have to cast imaginations down! Coz I've been there and done it, I know how it feels, so it can be a challenge!

I have conquered it! Do I do any of these things? Nope not any more! I deal with these issues with *INTEGRITY*, it's a test and we are all human beings FACT!

"Friend, it's okay to shout sometimes, okay to be angry sometimes, okay to cry, but sin not," it says in the Bible (God's Mind) keep your head up!

We all know association is important and we need to be careful who we let speak into our lives, I have friends that challenge me, and they encourage me on things and I can trust them.

My friends have helped build my character in Christ during my Christian walk! People like Curtis I remember when we talked we just clicked straight!

He used to give me a lot of sound advice and inspiration, then the soldier Curtis lead me to the path of God allowing himself, to be used as a tool of God, and Brothers not agreeing with everything I say or do! That's the kind of friends you need round you!

With the character I now have, I would offer my life as a living sacrifice for my family or anyone to get "salvation".

Backsliding, don't faze me anymore coz I recognise who I am in Christ. Even If I feel I want to backslide I can't, that character just ain't in me anymore. There were countless times I ran from integrity coz I didn't feel I could carry the responsibility yet, *but when are we really ready?*

The fact is we have to be ready now and realise everything is a process and God needs to use you as you are and will buck up with you where you are! You can't run from the truth, Jackson, my brothers especially, they know the truth and they are accountable and I believe God will use these young men to do exploits, I love those guys dearly!

The character of Jesus is imbedded in me and can be imbedded in you too! I'm about my fathers business all over these sheets of paper, being my brother's keeper. Paying the price!

I feel bad when I think about it, I actually used to tell girls I don't really want a relationship just sex, bad in it. God builds your character, and can change your character! You must believe me by now reading all the jazz I've been through!

Let some aggression out on the devil with prayer!

It's funny some people think when you take Christianity serious you lose your identity and become a boring person, that you don't joke anymore, have fun, have a dry face, dry hands, bad breath, dry hair, I'm hear to tell you its not true, like I said before. I still wear designer clothes, but use clean money, I smell good, really and truly I still look the same but my spirit has completely change. Just coz you decide to become Christian don't mean you're perfect either, just coz you stop smoking, drinking, sleeping around, and give to the poor, don't make you better than anyone else.

But the fact of the matter is when you get God's character, *INTEGRITY,* something has to change, you can't continue to beat people up, threaten people, kill people, sleep around having sex with everything in sight out of wedlock (marriage), getting drunk out of your head, smoking your brains out, killing thousands of brain cells, constantly cussing everything and everyone, lying and stealing! *You gots to change.*

<u>Romans chapter 12 verse 2 reads:</u> Be transformed by the renewing of your mind.

1 Corinthians chapter 13 verse 1 says: *without love I am nothing!*

"I am jack" without love! That's integrity and true character, L -o- v- e!

Friends ask me why don't I go raving anymore? I am basically staying away from temptations, I may be tempted to drink, smoke, and chat someone up! Paul puts it this way in **Romans chapter 7 verse 18**: In my flesh, my mortal and carnal body nothing good dwells in me.

God automatically builds character! Check this scriptures out: **1Colossians chapter 2 verse 16, 1Colossians chapter 3verse 3.**

How can you just see someone and judge them coz of how they look, don't think it's just you, it happens to the best of us, God created you for a purpose to worship, love and succeed! In other words *"do exploits!*

Everytime I get angry now, I realise within seconds where God has brought me from! Even in the little things like no longer stealing and fighting. I have passed my driving test, I now pay for petrol like everybody else, and pay for my car insurance, tax and mot.

Christians (Christ Like People) are not always happy, but fight to be always happy by taking authority through God's Word! Friend there is another way, friend you don't have to sell drugs, friend you don't have to end up dead, friend you don't have to give up! The integrity of God is here!

"I was just thinking, 'I make myself laugh' sometimes, everytime I eat, I pray late these days it happens everyday, coz I'm always in a hurry, immediately as I take my first bite I stop and thank God for my food and pray. *"I give myself joke sometimes"*.

Friend you are somebody, friend you can have a peace, friend it is not easy, friend through God Jesus to Christ everything is possible.

Friend don't be afraid or ashamed bout your past! Friend if you're not going to pay the price forget it!

Friend you are valuable. Be ready to pay the price by fighting the fight to stay righteous, submitting is a good way to begin unlocking your blessing! Friend don't dilly, dally and beat round the bush, friend don't forget your dreams and your visions friend be positive!

Matthew chapter 20 verse 16: *"So the last will be first, and the first last. For many are called, but few are chosen!"* Who is chosen? You are chosen friend, if you trust in God! Many are not chosen because they do not have full faith, according to **John chapter 15 verse 16** in God's Mind and believe they are not chosen so they stay not chosen.

You must believe you are "chosen" to be "chosen".

John chapter 15 verse 16 It does carry a responsibility though!

Check this out: **Philippians chapter 3 verse 12 13 14 15 6**

Waiting for my breakthrough, waiting for a break through can seem hard sometimes, but the key is to stand on the faith, speak it, thank God for it, believe it, receive it, and wait for it!

Because I had one thing wrong certain times, I was waiting for a particular prayer to manifest.

I had to reprogram and start from the bottom by doing things now legally, proper, clean money, forgiving, and stop complaining. We can delay our breakthrough by unbelief, and left over sin that is not dealt with, some people don't even realise that! *"I didn't before, now I do, though!*

"I keep going on about it but it's a fact nobody is perfect!

When I get angry these days, or broke, or irritated, or go through trials, I realise quickly what is happening, coz I have grown spiritually, and pray and repent in my mind! People are afraid of holiness.

"We need to get with the programme"

Renew your mind, you need to get to the level where you minister to yourself! Coz the Holy Spirit dwells in you!

"Jesus reveals God's character" that's deeeeeeep.

Ephesians chapter 4 verse 29: *"let no corrupt word proceed out of your mouth, but what is good for necessary edification, that may impart grace to the hearers.*

Swearing and cussing, ain't right bro! It pollutes!

Hosea chapter 4 verse 6: *My people are destroyed by lack of knowledge. Because* you have rejected knowledge, I also will reject you from being a priest for Me. Because you have forgotten the law of your God, I also will forget your children.

Lack of knowledge! Lack of knowledge, lack of knowledge, lack of knowledge! *Knowledge here is talking bout God,* knowledge is God and worshiping Him! Lack of God people die because of what they require, what they need, what they should have, who is God but the outcome of not receiving and worshiping God is un-protection.

Your kids and your family who don't know God will not be protected or Blessed until they accept God or you accept God, you have nothing to lose bro, God ain't harsh He is fair and wants you to chose Him and His will. God loves everyone He is waiting for you.

Joshua chapter 1 verse 8: *"This Book of the Law shall not depart from your mouth, but you shall meditate in it day and night, that you may observe to do according to all that is written in it. For then you will make your way prosperous, and then you will have good success.*

Keep in constant prayer and reading the Word! (The Bible)

People are at different places and different levels spiritually!

Chapter 18

Hardened Heart

People like to say: *"All this religion thing is rubbish"*, excuses, excuses, excuses, nobody ain't forcing no one to do *NISH*!

As I said before we all have choices. "I say a little prayer for you buddy. Some people don't want to realise, recognise or accept Jesus Christ but you know what, it's okay. It's true He walked the earth, and lived but I ain't even gonna lecture you mate I'll let you decide what you want to do. I pray God softens your heart.

A lot of people don't want the truth coz they feel Jesus ain't done jack for them, but not realised He did! He died on the cross for us! Why? He had to fulfil prophecy and put right what man did wrong i.e. Adam. God told Adam, not to touch the tree of knowledge or he will die if he did!

God could not go back on His word coz whatever God says happens, God's word is *ACTION*! I was baffled when I first read this coz I thought why ain't Adam dead yet? Coz Adam had many kids and lived till he was about *900* and something years old. *"Bingo"* 'I got a revelation God meant death, as in, face hell with the devil, where the devil was, the fallen angel with his own corruption! And all man/woman was going there if they were in sin, which was death!

Jesus died to save us from the sin and death (eternal damnation).

God lived as man to offer His blood as a living sacrifice for all our sins and save us from death, so we could chill with him in heaven (paradise) I had doubts before, coz I could not see, feel, or touch God, so I got wound up!

I thought why did God let this person or that person die? The truth is every one has to die one day. But some may have just been at the wrong place at the wrong time, walking in sin, which means *death forever,* some maybe Christians died coz they may have fulfilled their destiny. What ever the deal is people have died.

Wouldn't you want to secure your eternity by making sure your cool when you leave your body? Coz you have a spirit you know! Where does that go when you die? The gift of God is eternal life! The wages of sin is death. So by accepting God's gift (Grace/Eternal Life of Peace) you are rejecting death (hell) when you die, but by accepting sin you accept death (Hell).

There are some people you can't help coz, they need to first help themselves first. Wake up, God calls all the time but it's up to people to acknowledge Him and make a decision, God is a gentleman!

It is awesome when you activate that Greater Thing in you. That Greater Thing is peace, Jesus, God and it is noticed all though you may not see it. God is real!!

It's funny coz I couldn't stand the truth sometimes or face it, sometimes it took me longer to give up smoking drugs, sleeping around and crime coz I was always in the association of people who did that, in **Proverbs chapter 13 verse 20:** says there is power in association, if you hang with wise men you will be wise, if you hang with fools you will be foolish, now with God when you have a relationship with Him you get 'understanding' that the Bible is the mind of God, now it depends if you feel you are strong enough to be a light amongst darkness and share the peace, and love of Jesus if not then your choking and polluting your spirit mind, and destiny, coz the company you keep determines part of your destiny and lifestyle.

One can't be forced to live for God, *believe*!

My friend René once said something deep, and true: "God helps those that help themselves". *Now that is true "boomer",* coz sometimes I get vex when I feel like I Just can't help myself.

How can I tell you to do something that I have not experienced or been through?

You are reading about a young man who's experienced what he's talking about. We all come across people who don't seem to have manners, and just don't wanna hear what you have got to say.

I remember when I first started evangelising,

I walked up to a middle aged guy and asked him if he knew who Jesus was and he just continued to walk past me in ignorance and said: "Who doesn't". I feel that was selfishness, some people are so stingy, so tight, their bum squeaks!

A lot of people, unbelievers, hold a lot of bitterness, anger, stress etc, which could be about the system, job, partner, being hurt, cheated, robbed, abused, being beaten up, a death, being poor, anything, but we need to blame someone! So what do we do? Blame God and reject Him! Is that wise? God as man Jesus was spat on, beaten up, stabbed, betrayed, abused, robbed, cheated, but did He hold bitterness anger or rejection? "NO".

I know it ain't always easy, it can be easier said than done. But we have to let it go.

Should you forgive and forget? **Yes!**

Simple! Some people or an enemy who made you angry, are having a fantastic time coz they may have repented and felt guilty already and have long forgot on what they did to hurt you, it's the last thing on their mind!

We hold it in by holding a grudge.

I'm not saying we can't be angry coz I've been guilty of this many times but guess what? *I let it go*! So why suffer and miss out on loads of things God has in store for you, get on with your life man!

Faith, faith, faith. I've mentioned faith a couple of times already, but I want to get this message across to you! Faith is a revelation, is a testimony, it is character, it is nature, it is personality, it is real, it is Power, and it is integrity!

Psalm Chapter 14 Verse 1: *A fool says in his heart, there is know God!*

What are you gonna do when your credits run out?

Your life is like a pay as you go phone, the credits are from the Word (God's Mind, The Bible) and when we don't access The Word we become dry and unable to react in a powerful way.

I have learnt life is about choices for instance, as Christians we need to get of our behind and share the love, the Word (God's Mind, The Bible).

How to go about it is by self-motivation with help from the Holy Spirit and put it into action. We should be walking in love not condemnation.

We should be Blessed not Cursed.

I can't ram the Bible, Jesus, and God down your throat, or try to force you to listen.

The best thing is to pray and be led by the Spirit!

To seek God's truth and get to a revelation, you simply have to read the Bible (God's Mind) and pray to Him by talking to Him, as you would talk to a person normally. You ain't "crackers" coz God is very real!

"Whatever you do please read these verses in the Bible (God's Mind)

Hebrews chapter 3 verses 7 8 9 10 11 12 13 14 15.

Why harden your heart? Listen to God's call and obey.

We try to ignore His voice, we hear it but reject it and harden our heart. I hardened my heart before, but when I submitted it to God and asked Him questions I found the answers in Him.

If you obey God you will profit, so *please stop hardening your heart. At the end of the day it's all about Jesus!*

YOU HAVE TO RECOGNIZE WHO YOU ARE IN CHRIST

God deals with you

God says rebellion is like witchcraft.

Ephesians Chapter 5 Verse 6 Let no one deceive you with vain words, get out of the darkness, get into the light and stay in the light.

"AS A PERSON THINKS IN HIS HEART SO IS HE" It says this in the Bible (God's Mind) research this scripture.

If you're negative God said: Out of the abundance of the heart the mouth speaks so be careful of what you say....

Please stop hardening your heart. I feel your pain. We've all be through things.

If you take a moment to look at your life you can ACTUALLY SEE what the Lord God has done throughout your life, in situations, issues and circumstances.

HE HAS DONE GREAT THINGS, WOULDN'T YOU AGREE?

These Chapters and scriptures are for you to read:

Psalms chapter 91 verse 1-

Deuteronomy chapter 28 verse 13-

Daniel chapter 11 verse 32-

Hebrews chapter 4 verse 12-

Isaiah Chapter 55 Verse 11-

"Whatever you do you have to read this chapter in the Bible (God's Mind)

Luke Chapter 15 Verse 11 a good example of a backslider "The prodigal son"

Please unhardened your heart, please friend....

Chapter 19

Seasons & Questions

Have I felt God's presence? Yep, I have. My entire life has changed, I went from being lost to found, being a criminal, to a Christian (Christ Like Person) so can you!

I did this by taping into God's presence. He touched me coz I cried out to Him, I believe when an individual swallows his/her pride and surrenders and opens up to God, *through prayer, God meets you where you're at and He touches you.*

You will be able to feel God by making a conscious decision to allow Him to take control by touching you.

When I felt God's presence it felt like I don't know? Coz words can't describe, the closest word is *"Awesome"*, God's presence is heavy it feels like the smoothest silk gliding all over your body, it's just peace, *"PEACE MAN"*.

I have been in God's presence many times. And when I am I usually feel light, and when I try to open my eyes sometimes I can't, or if I do I just see a blur or just white, it feels like I'm moving in slow motion, and it feels like I am floating, *"It's Brilly Man"*.

In God's presence is truly the fullness of joy God's presence is eternal.

Everyone can have different experiences of God's presence, but most people who have felt God's presence have felt similar feelings.

I can't stop talking bout it. It feels potent it's like silk and pure air gliding inside and outside of your body. I sometimes feel like I am about to take off and fly like superman. It is a great experience to feel God's touch.

The last Experience I recall I was in His presence for about 20 minutes but it felt like I was in God's presence for 2 minutes, then I would start shaking for about another *20 minutes,* it feels like you're being massaged in a non describable way, it feels like your drunk nearly, it feels good.

Trust me to get to that level you have just got to want it and cry out to Him, physically stretching your arms, soul and all, reach out to Him with your eyes closed.

When I feel that presence I feel like laughing, crying, shouting, rejoicing and thanking God all at the same time! Bro, Bro, Bro it's *"HEAVY"* I have only felt this about six, seven times strongly, but actually mind you, when I'm worshipping God in song, I feel God's presence and it feels like what I just said but not always as strong.

I suppose, God's presence is more evident when I have been delivered, or set free, or when I let go, letting loose, expressing myself to God. Also when I feel upset, repentant, hurt, tested, lonely or just liberated, the presence of God is truly peace and joy! God to says to cast all your burdens to Him.

In the presence of God is fullness of joy! Worship Jesus and you will feel it too it's that simple!

Just tap into that presence of God! God ain't far away He is right there!

From feeling the presence of God I can slightly imagine how Moses felt at the burning bush. He could never be the same again. He was physically standing on Holy ground in God's presence.

Read: **Exodus chapter 3**

This might seem like a load of pie in the sky but I know what I am talking about.

"Deal with it, deal with the matter!

A wreck like me, turned into a 'True Solider for Christ' .

I can truly say I have a peace! *You say how can I have peace when I still have trials and tribulation?* "I have, coz the *"peace"* is a promise and a one-way ticket to Heaven.

Pure faith *"Evidence"* of what has been said in His Word (The Bible) (God's Mind)

If you take bits of anything you can easily take it out of context. You can destroy and slander it.

There are people out there that are on a mission to cause confusion. A lot of these people go out of their way to destroy the truth and find bits and bobs, of the Word in the Bible to twist, which can get people into a limbo, there are many negative people out there who find minor excuses to attack the truth.

"Bro the truth shall set you free!!!!!

A simple argument like this for example: **John Chapter 3 verse 16**: "*For God so love the world that He gave His only begotten Son, that whoever believes in Him should not perish but have everlasting life!*

You may say: "so if someone doesn't believe, are you saying they will not be saved and go to heaven aye?

That is true, but then you may say God does not Love but then again He has given us all a choice!

He does love, so why would it be a contradiction? God ain't bypassed people.

People can misunderstand God if you do not know His true character.

"The wages of sin is death but the gift of God is eternal life.

Why would God want us to *"DIE"* then?

He doesn't He said the consequences of *"SIN"* is *"DEATH"*. So He wants us to reject *"SIN"* by *"FAITH"*.

If we choose His *"GIFT"* which is *"LIFE"*, His Grace and Jesus, we will escape *"DEATH"*, which is *"HELL"* and *"SIN"*. Like I explained before!

You might then say 'oh hypocrite', contradiction, a lie, not true, see it there.

Friend hold up, just a minute! Lets address the issue why you say God is a hypocrite? Friend we need *UNDERSTANDING* (God sent His son into the world not to condemn it, but to give life more and more and more and more abundantly).

You may still question so why does it say in the (Old Testament) this and that and in the (New Testament) this and that?

"Well that's why God Almighty sent Jesus Christ to lay down the new foundations and doctrines and new laws i.e., His lifestyle.

Sacrifices and burnt offerings we see from the *(Old Testament)* Jesus laid down all the kosher foundations and laws through all the disciples, Paul and John plus other various Christ followers have continued to expand on Jesus Christ's foundations.

It was like cruising through the *(Old Testament)* in the Bible, you see the old rules and laws, then Jesus Christ came and established, and laid down the final rules and laws and when you match things up it all makes sense in the end. *GOD SENT HIS WORD*

John Chapter 1 Verse 1
We don't run to the farm to get a goat or lamb for sin offering for God it would seem very insane in this day and age. Jesus came and died to be the final sacrifice. He has just simply said confess our sins openly to one another and He will forgive! It's all grace and mercy it's simple *GRACE.*

We are all humans at the end of the day and we make mistakes.

God is more real than my "Timberland boots".

"We all go through hard times, bad times, and good times. In the midst of it all we need to just receive the will of God for our lives!

This is my prayer everyday *"Lord create in me a clean heart"*, when I couldn't even carry on with this book and I went through so much pain, betrayal, depression, horror, tragedy, shock, anger, bitterness, hurt, a broken spirit and experienced what *longsuffering really* meant in that scripture and chapter in the book of **Galatians chapter 5 verse 22**. It was a challenge but I dealt with it!

As I said it's not me writing this book it is the Holy Spirit working in me it's not a carnal thing, this is another form of ministry.

My God kept me. After all the scars of life, hurt and pain, *I wanna tell and reassure you, everything will be okay!"* I didn't do it by myself it was that Greater thing in me that I had activated, that kept me going and pulled me through, only Jesus not me.

I keep promoting God and His name coz He is so mighty and loving!

Not spending enough time in God's presence causes you to leak, I sometimes just make a decision you know what. *It's all about me (Teslim) and God.* Things will challenge your faith. I ask you: "Have you ever had a dream? I'm willing to pay the price, I got a record deal it didn't go all the way through 'so what' I have peace!

What if what you're praying for doesn't come? Will you still be strong till the end? Coz you have prayed and nothing has changed does not mean God has not heard you.

Psalm chapter 14 verse 1: *A fool says in his heart, there is no God!!!*

You can get to know or figure out God's character it's simple Keep the zeal and stay focused in the will of God!

"I know God's Character"

Chapter 20

Testify!

Testifying means *'Giving Evidence'*, life is full of surprises! Take it for what it's worth my birth is a blessing. Your birth is a Blessing!

Principles of life you always reap what you sow,

You runaway from God but yet His mercy and His grace! Endures forever, its always available *24 hours a day*, stop rejecting it. We all qualify for a blessing. I go through stuff daily we all do, and it's like who can you trust?

Friend only God almighty! **1 John Chapter 2 Verse 27** *God is calling you to use you for His glory!* I'm in tha struggle too, but the difference is I choose how I struggle.

A lot of people I have looked up to, have let me down' one way or the other'.

The pastor I called my pastor till year *2002* let me down, friends, church, uncle, family have let me down too. The only person that can't is God. God can't let me down!

Playing Church And Kingdom Business

I see a lot of people who play church but you can only play church and pretend to be Christian for a season! *'YOU'RE PLAYING YOURSELF BOOMER'.*

Motto the Word is POWERFUL life and death is in tha power of tha tongue! Tha Word carries weight, effect, efficacy, potential and power.

False Prophets And Ear Teasers

Learn to be teachable and beware of wolves in sheep's clothing!

Please, please, please, please read: Matthew chapter *24* verse

5 Ephesians chapter *5* verse *6*

Daniel chapter *11* verses *32*

Timothy chapter *2* verse *3*

Timothy chapter *2* verse *15*

I used to get upset before, just coz I didn't own my favorite car, or achieve a particular goal in life which was to be able to provide for my parents and stop them from working. I don't get upset any more, but the dream is still there, our dreams and visions keep us going. I will keep dreaming and I will get my Cherokee jeep one day, and I will be able to provide for my parents one day and take them shopping, and release my own clothing label.

I used to think about just money, I wanted wealth before but that don't matter no more it's all about my peace now, God and my dreams and achieving it!

You have to trust the Lord's Word! No matter what that is your strength!

"If I could rewind time I wouldn't, I've seen so much, learned so much, experienced so much. It has made me a stronger and more rooted person. And it has made me who I am today. I would not have wanted to go through all the trials I have been through at a later date I am glad I've been through it now.

When I sinned, I sinned well, now I am a Christian I have to be good at it!

It's all faith............

Name Brand Gospel!!

Someone needs reprogramming if you're vexed or irritated or convicted sorry but it's tha Word.

In church these days I have seen and experienced *'Church politics'* homemade rules and made up doctrine's **Hebrews Chapter 13 Verse 9-** God talks about all these issues and strange tings coz people are getting confused!

When you hear about all these fake Christians, hypocrites.

God clearly states all these things will go on. Look out all you have got to do is study to show yourself approved, when you meditate and study the fullness of God, things happen and wisdom kicks in.

The Bible (God's Mind) God gave to us as our guideline, which shows us things such as, stories, tests, lessons and examples of situations, with REAL PEOPLE!

Everything in this Bible, The Bible REVEALS EVERYTHING!

WE ALL FACE SPIRITUAL WARFARE, open your Spiritual eyes the battle against good and evil starts!

Write down on a piece of paper God is good!

Research the Word (The Bible) look up words and use a dictionary, thesaurus and a concordance. Go deep face the challenge.

God has told us where we're going, and what is happening, God reveals all these things to us!

It's All 'Grace' & Mercy! It's All 'Grace' & Mercy!

I say to you: "ask, seek, knock".

When God said ask it shall be given He ain't joking about you know He has actually given, He ain't gonna give to you again, coz He can't, He has already said it is given so it is given?

What is given?

Whatever desires you're asking for, when you keep asking you have no knowledge or understanding it is there, I must admit I forget sometimes, but realise quick and think what am I doing?

The Holy Spirit prompts me, then I change my words and just say thank you to God and hold on to the belief!

So the next time when you knock, know that the door is open all you have got to do is walk through it, walk in your blessing. When you seek know that you will find it believe stand on God's Word, God does not lie, it ain't my words!

Know that when you seek you have really found what you are looking for! It's there made available from God so enjoy the benefits of it take the next step of acting in faith. *ACTION!*

The key to getting a blessing is to keep living right, by God's Word, thank and worship in advance, you have to do this daily until you see it!

Feeding And Teaching

What are you allowing into your spirit?

Being a 'Pastor' means big responsibility, coz you're taking care of other people's spiritual needs! You have to be watchful that the world is not coming into the church when the church is meant to be going into the world. *STOP, LOOK AND LISTEN!*

We can have fun in the church but we need to be real with the Word of God.

I have come across many false prophets using flattering words to get you to give! That's *WRONG*, feeling pressured to give is *WRONG!*

Positions getting to peoples head, *getting all puffed up. That's where it crashes and gets blown out of portion!*

I feel a lot of leaders are going astray from the Word and get all arrogant, rude and offensive without even knowing it, coz they are far-gone. God can't fully use Crap.

We need to get it right with the new covenants and old covenants for *example the Sabbath day and Tithing a basic example and foundation. God is not a respecter of persons. 'God wants us to know that all things belongs to Him. All I am, all I have, not just 10%, 20% whatever percent it's all God's....*

Getting led astray and drawn into false doctrines and all that crap is a shame, I have been through it and *personally I am sick of it!*

We need JUICE (Preachers and ministers with juice) we need SUBSTANCE (preachers and ministers with substance) of the Word of God!

'Stand still' and let God speak to you. "The problem with a lot of us Christians, is laziness, *'It stinks'*. We need to stop running to the evangelist, preacher, or pastor for direction, revelation, healing or prayer everytime.

There must be some spiritual maturity after a while. *"Yeah we should not lean on our own understanding and be sensitive to the Holy Spirit and all that jazz.*

But after being a Christian a few months, a year, two years we need to grow up spiritually and start to seek God for ourselves knowing our *MINISTRY AND PURPOSE! Grow up!*

I get most of my revelation when I'm bathing, I think that's when I'm most relaxed coz I'm not *"busy bodying around"* I am a busy body, we all are but we need to just *STAND STILL!* Sometimes.

This is a vital key we need to seek God and digest His Word and Will.

When you go to the gym and pump some weights you need to give your body a one or two day rest and then go again, just like eating we are hungry so we eat until we are full and let it digest. The same with God save yourself from being rumbled and shipwrecked! Choose to live well.

Acts Chapter 20Verse 28, 2 Timothy Chapter 2 Verse 15

Stand Still...

My Philosophy!

It's sickening when I look around me, I can see there's a high percent of churches not lining up with the Word! So much false prophets, the lack of impact we are making, we can do more. We have got to rise up and make a stand, a conscious decision! By making a change 'its all love'.

Far too much compromise, a lot of Christians in a comfort zone it's all long!

Words are blown out of portion or taken out of context not much seems to be lining up with the Word. We need to go back to basics! *Love, a compassionate heart, an humble and contrite heart, worship, Serving!*

I was baffled for a while when I was writing all these things down and unhappy with myself. Then I asked myself what am I doing to make a stand? Well I was searching and standing on the truth, the Word the Bible (God's Mind)

When the Spirit moves, it moves, coz where the Spirit of God is there is liberty! *"Believe that!* Greater is He that's in us. Where's the Unity at? I feel we need to get a hold of this unity thing in the body of Christ and get our acts together!

This conviction should be burning, or you are weak and not working out your salvation with fear and trembling lacking tha Word!

Time to stop tha compromise! Time to stop tha dilution!

It's all about the Word without compromising it! The truth offends, but the truth brings clarity, direction, and guidance. No one's telling anyone to change, but I'm asking though, coz God's Word teaches and corrects, so we need to get into it people!

"ATTENTION". The Love of God changes people.

The Word of God carry's weight and the Holy Spirit is *POWERFUL.*

So lets walk in the Spirit *shall we?* And stop lacking the Word. What we feed our spirit mind is what we get out of it.

You may be baffled a bit and think well I thought the Holy Spirit is from God so why do we need to feed the Holy Spirit, well you are correct, the Holy Spirit is God so we have to put it into operation by acknowledging Him. The way we do that is by reading our Bible, prayer and worship! We control how we walk in the Spirit so we have to put time into it!

Exposure

The company you keep can affect your destiny. People and friends around you need to be real you need a friend that you can trust, a true friend._If you are continuing to sin willfully you are not a genuine Christian. If you commit a sin or do wrong things and you are never guilty or you never feel bad you don't fear God you are not a Christian.

You must be in the will of God. I'm not judging you but what makes you so special? What makes you special that you can escape hell when living in sin? You can know the mind of God you don't need a Pastor to keep telling you! The Word of God corrects!

Silver or gold or Jesus? What is the point gaining the world but losing you soul? *I agree silly init.*

The Bible (God's Mind) contains scandals, killers, homosexuals, and pornography talks of people like Muhammad, Buddha, Harry Krishna, Rasta's and Gandhi who were also born of a sinful nature descendant of Adam. All these other claimed prophets or leaders were not born of the Holy Spirit they were not raised from the dead. If Mary were not really a virgin when she had Jesus we would have found out about that by now!

Read **Romans chapter 1 verse 17-32**

Code1: *Let it go, forgive and forget, coz if you don't the person may have forgot and you're torturing yourself, by being angry for nothing.*

Code2: *Keep your values and integrity.*

Code3: *Don't think you are special or better than anybody else. God does not have a favourite person!*

To The Man Dem!

A *real man will fear God*

A real man will face responsibility

A *real man is grateful*

A real man realises his faults

A *real man repents*

A real man loves

A *real man has integrity*

A real man gives

A *real man prays*

A real man worship's God almighty

A *real man walks by faith and not by sight*

A real man cries

Shalom (Peace)

Chapter 21

Magic Team

The 'magic team' is when two become 'one'.

Are you searching for that virtuous woman or man?

Virtuous means: righteous, good, worthy, moral, upright, and honest. When you search the devil can trick and interfere here, so let God do it by chasing God, seek God and you will know when you have met that person by divine connection that will form the magic team!

The spirit connects when you both click or make a move faith without works is dead.

Remember men choose their wife women don't choose their husband but at the same time to incorporate understanding if a woman likes a man and the man responds then it's all good, but if a man is not responding and getting on with it don't claim the man. You must either be patient or move on by serving God.

I believe it's not all about being segregated, and isolated with just our own race or culture or being old fashioned. Culture barriers need to be broken, as long as it's genuine love, love is love!

Understand God can give you wisdom to find the right wife, right husband, and right job! It's important to have good friends around you, friends who tell the truth and can pray with you. It would be nice if they could challenge you too we all have to stir up each other's gifts, exercising faith putting faith into practice.

Remember nobody is perfect! There is a strong hold in the church amongst the Christians when it comes to marriages.

I strongly feel as a Christian, you should date/court with the intention to marry.

We are not of the world but yet some let Hollywood, the society and the media dictate what the right partner man/woman, husband or wife should be like.

We need to follow God's plan and not be confirmed to this world. If the (Biblical) qualities are there lets get it together. God's will for us is to be in unity that is where God commands the Blessing. Amen

Not much marriages why?

The Holy Spirit gave me a revelation that there is a strong hold in the churches amongst the single Christians when it comes to marriages.

People are not making no moves I.E men *"come on"* stop being afraid of a rejection or your circumstances.

There is this idea single Christian men and women have which needs to be broken. Which is in order to step to the marriage realm you must have loads of wealth and prosperity to bring to a marriage.

We don't have to wait to be on a huge salary or the big fully paid house to get married. It would help though but make the moves and watch God make a way! He is in control when you put Him in control!

The main qualities and wealth you should be bringing to a marriage is 'Agape Behaviour', and God's qualities and expectations highlighted in the Holy Bible (The Mind Of God) 1 Corinthians chapter 7, Hebrews chapter 13 verse 4, Proverbs chapter 18 verse 22 and Ephesians chapter 5 verse 22 - 33.

I am a young man who desires a woman in my life and being real I enjoy sex, but sex out of the will of God (God's Plan) was never intended.

Sex is not everything, SEX (making love, intercourse, intimacy) is something that is SACRED and is meant for enjoyment. That is why God created it. But He (God) intended SEX for *MARRIAGE*. As I said before somewhere in this book sex/sleeping around with different people produces paranoia and confusion, on top of that you could get a disease!

Eros (Greek For Sexual Type Of Love)

1. Sex out of God's will produces unwanted desires

2. (Confusion/paranoia), past experiences flashbacks, lust

3. Unwanted/unplanned pregnancy, unwanted disease and unwanted responsibility

4. You pay the penalty and the price of bad or wrong choices. You always reap the consequences, because you want short-term satisfaction, fulfilment and pleasure

5. At the end you incur 'no peace', *"not what you are really looking for"*, so you still feel incomplete.

The Wrong Way: Advantages: None

Disadvantages: a whole lot plus you can die catching a disease

Sex in God's will produces peace, security, satisfaction, fulfilment, pleasure and contentment long term.

The Right Way: Advantages: a whole lot plus you don't die catching a disease from your spouse, you feel right and you enjoy it more.

Disadvantages: None.

Sexual sin comes when we follow our own plan which leads to confusion, paranoia, and people falling away under condemnation so lets bring God's foundation back.

Sex out of God's will is never beneficial, if you have sex out of God's will you will suffer the consequences, however God will still restore you if you get back into His will and plan.

When you have sex with someone you are becoming one with that person! That's why it is hard to move on mentally and spiritually after you have broken up with someone you have had sex with who you were not married to. Coz a part of you is connected to that person still. But you can be set free from this damage, by seeking God, prayer and fasting and totally disconnecting, friendship, relationship and conversation with that person.

There is no time period on when a man makes a choice to propose as long as there is enough knowledge, vibes of feeling the same way and most importantly true LOVE. Not just Eros (sexual Love) make sure all types of love is there, then you could marry in three months to a year but don't delay and waste time if you are in the will of God.

If you do delay make sure it is to see or test for fruit (character and integrity). Nobody is perfect. The world tells us to try out different sexual fantasies God says to look for the fruits of the Spirit, virtue and integrity! **Galatians chapter 5 verse 22** talks about the fruits of the Spirit.

Check out what happened to King David in The Bible (God's Mind) in: **(2 Samuel chapter 11 -, Psalms chapter 51)**, Samson and Delilah: **(Judges chapter 16)**,

Jezebel: **(1 King chapter 16 verse 31 -, chapter 19)**, the Jezebel spirit: **(Revelation chapter 2 verse 20).**

Joseph: **(Genesis chapter 39 verse 7)** was the only man who did the right thing till the end, which paid off ABUNDANTLY.

I personally wanted to be in God's will but as a young Christian I fell over many times in the area of sexual sin, why?

I was not walking in the fullness of the fruit of the SPIRIT. But as I grew Spiritually in the things of God I knew that I knew that I had to be right in the sight of God, and follow His plan.

So when I found the lady I made a choice. The choice was to be right in the sight of God and get to know this person, so I made the **First Step:** Dinner dating and going to the cinema as much times as possible. (Go on as many dates as possible, so you can learn each other's character and reactions, allowing issues and situations to come up, to see how you both react when you both are angry, happy, busy, lonely and sad).

Take precautions, don't put yourself in a predicament where you can fall or mess up 'Holy Matrimony', don't stay the night at each other's house or stay in each other's company where you are both left alone where both of you could loose control. If you both really love each other you will obey God and wait for each other and do it the best way, coz the best way pays off.

Step Two: As time went on I felt this would be the lady I could make my wife so I popped the question. And I proposed with a nice diamond ring.

Step Three: I knew that I knew I had strong feelings but I did not have my own place, a huge salary, but I was in the will of God, all the qualities where there so I trusted God and I **set a date!**

Step Four: I went to the hospital clinic with my partner to get tested for any infections or disease (Physically) and then asked God to search me, clean me and order my steps (Spiritually). If you are going to walk right take the right precautions and do the right thing!

If you have the desire to be with a man/woman marry, marry and be in unity then let God command the **BLESSING!** (I made a 'CHOICE' I wanted to love this lady, God' s way) it's the heart condition and motive God sees.

Remember marriage is hard work, it's not a happy ever after story, you still have to 'get to know' and 'understand' your spouse, it's a blessing. It is God's love for us.

The Bible says he that finds '*A WIFEY FINDS A GOOD THING AND OBTAINS FAVOUR FROM GOD*'.

Proverbs chapter 18 verse 22

Don't mess up 'Holy Matrimony'

Let us break this strong hold **Amen!**

Chapter 22

OVERSTANDING

Over-understanding! The Bible is a library, a catalogue of the great men and women "God used specially" *to show us examples and lessons to learn from! The Bible (God's Mind) contains knowledge, facts, science, how to eat, drink, get a partner, get money, love, integrity, understanding, wisdom, power, peace, and the way of life!*

Jesus, and all the events and the actions that took place, God specifically chose all these things we read about for a purpose and reason. I believe to inspire encourage and test! There could have been tons and tons of past events that took place, that God could have lead people to finalise and put in the Bible (God's Mind) but He put everything in THE HOLY BIBLE exactly the way it is for a purpose.

God shared His mind and actions from beginning to end "is that not an honour?"

It tells me God wants us to know the truth and have life abundantly. Through His Word, He intended us all to know His will, character, love, mercy, sovereignty, grace, power, events, lessons, promises, plans, peace and heaven! God's plans for us are for good and not evil!

God wants to give you life and give you that life more abundantly my friend. *He wants you to live in heaven forever in peace!*

The phone line to Jesus is open seven days a week twenty-four hours a day.

"There is something about the name Jesus there is power and peace" I challenge you to try using his name sincerely I dare you!

Use that name in your trials, in your situations, in your issues, in your struggles. How do you think heaven is gonna be when you get there? It is gonna be good, the finest gold you could ever imagine will be there, there will be pure love, no competition, no pain, no devil to tempt or mess with you.

The devil is going to be destroyed he is the father of lies. His character is stealing, killing, deceit, fornication, lies, confusion, anger the master of wickedness and badness.

The fool and thief called satan/lucifer the devil, enjoys trying to kill real God Chasers! He wants to stop you knowing the truth and going with God's flow. The devil will wait all your life to take you out, coz he has got all that time to wait. He will keep trying to do you something and if it don't work he will keep trying, and trying until he can do something to attack you! When he has the slightest access it's easy for him to mess with you but again Greater is He in you, he cannot harm you!

There is no such thing as luck. It is a subsidiary of faith it's weak faith, or being blunt fake faith!

Faith in Jesus is the correct faith, honour God, honour God first and He will Bless you. If you don't He still will Bless you, wow what mercy and grace.

Are you ready to handle the Blessing? Can you trust God through it all, and can God trust you yet?

Press In!

Over-understanding! Real men can cry, I need encouragement at times, and I definitely need stirring up too. I'm not always on a high with God I get down sometimes. I don't want you to think I am always happy coz I ain't sometimes I am miserable, but I'm **Blessed** though!

The devil gets me down sometimes but, it's all good coz I am an overcomer and he is a minor and he does not want me to catch him coz if we buck up I'll bang him up! *"For sure".*

Draw near to God and He will draw near to you:

Get Your Bible out and read the following chapters and scriptures below from the Bible (The Mind of God) His powerful and wise Words.

2 Chronicles chapter 16 verse 9: *God wants to show Himself strong to you*

Chronicles chapter 7 verse 14: *Humble yourself and Pray*

Romans chapter 10 verse 9: *Confess and Believe*

Romans chapter 10 verse 13: Call His name and be saved

John chapter 3 verse 16: God Loved the world He sent Jesus to die for you

Acts chapter 4 verse 12: Only the name of Jesus can save you

Philippians chapter 2 verse 9 – 11: Every knee shall bow at the name of Jesus

Philippians chapter 4 verse 19: God will supply all your needs

Psalms chapter 103 verse 8: God is slow to anger and compassionate

Psalms chapter 24: The earth is the Lord's

Isaiah 45 verse 5 – 7: God is sovereign the ruler of everything

Acts chapter 1 verse 8: You can receive supernatural power from God

Hebrews chapter 4 verse 12: God's word is quick, powerful and sharp

Hebrews chapter 11 verse 1: Faith is God's promises of His word

Hebrews chapter 11 verse 6: Without faith you cannot please God

James chapter 2 verse 20: Without action faith is dead

James chapter 4 verse 6: God resists the proud but gives grace to humble people

James chapter 4 verse 8: Draw near to God and He will draw near to you

2 Corinthians chapter 12 verse 9: My Grace is sufficient for you says the Lord. His Grace is all you need.

Why Go Church?

I'll tell ya why fellowship, unity, encouragement, to stir up each other's faith and spirit, revelation, worship, and to uplift God. If we don't have a church or go to a church how are we going to grow strong in the things of God?

Anyone going through something trials needs deliverance or healing by the power of God's Word. There are people who have been struggling with issues all week coz they have been busy studying or working and need that encouragement in the faith.

Then there is the dying world out there, where are they gonna go? We need church so that we can be able to relate to everyone, so the conviction, faith and heart don't grow weak.

Every seed takes time to grow!

Bible references is important get some equipment.

Can you eat pork or not? Yes if you bless whatever you wanna eat in the name of Jesus, God honours that, coz we are living under grace. At the same time it's up to you what you eat as long as it's not another human being!

Drinking or smoking, we all know is bad for your health, it can cause cancer, lung disease and definitely damages your lungs and heart, but it don't affect you having a relationship or friendship with God if you are a smoker.

Something could be said about your relationship with God if you smoke in front of other Christians that have overcome it or dislike it! However, if you don't or can't give up that can be a problem.

You have to make a choice on that but it won't make you less or more spiritual.

Don't just take what I say check it out for yourself in the Mind of God study to show yourself approved. It's integrity, moral, truth and righteousness!

Over-understanding! We are all sinners, so we shouldn't be too quick to judge, I used to think that a smoker would not go to heaven, coz I had a crazy idea they must not fear God to continue smoking. On the other hand what's smoking got to do with going to heaven coz it's a pleasurable thing of the *'world'* we live in.

At the same time if we know it will damage our lungs, it's up to us to bare the consequences, I now know it ain't got *'squat'* to do with the fear of God.

Some people don't have the conviction that smoking ain't any harm, although it can cause cancer. So it's not about condemning a brother or sister about it. *Smoking is a bad habit though, and it stinks.* God is Love.

We all have liberty and freedom to do what we want!!!! As the Word (God's Mind) says everything is permitted but not everything will benefit you.

It says in the Bible (God's Mind) your body is a temple!

We are under the law of Christ now coz we are in Christ, we are new creations. We are not under the *"Mosaic law"* which was the (Old Testament) Moses' laws, which God gave to him. We are now in Christ, in His covenant, His Grace (Unmerited Favour/Underserved Favour).

However, it does not mean some of the (Old Testament) does not apply some things still do.

They are confirmed in the (New Testament) all the stuff that applies.

Don't do anything to cause your brother to stumble.

Romans Chapter 14 Verse 21 it says don't do anything or even eat or drink anything, which will offend or cause your brother to stumble, making your brethren fall or weak or backslide don't make *"your brother sin!*

Philippians chapter 4 verse 8: Meditate on whatever is right!

1 Corinthians chapter 10 verse 23: Not all things are beneficial for you.

Colossians chapter 2 verse 16 17 18 19 20 21 22: *"Says let no man judge you in meat, drink, food or Sabbath days it's all about JESUS!*

Why is your sin forgiven when you receive salvation?

"It is coz God said so, you are coming back to God to reunite with Him, knowing that it is because of Him you live, He made you!

It is good to come to God sincerely identifying we are sinners and put our hands up and surrender "saying okay I recognise You, I am a sinner. God sees that and that honours Him! Coz He wants us to recognise Him, after all He sent Jesus into the world to die for all of our sins and take them all away.

When we confess Jesus and repent as a sinner God can work in us through the Holy Spirit, which is the Holy Guider. How do we work out what is wise and what is not, what is righteous and what is not?

As I said earlier in this book your spiritual eyes open when you recognise you are a sinner and let Jesus into your heart. The Holy Spirit is then activated and you are on your way to heaven, all you've got to do is believe with your heart.

If you don't mean it then you're playing yourself!

Once you have recognised you're a sinner and recognise Jesus died for your sins, everytime we sin as a Christian and have a repented heart that's cool, coz its an act of righteousness praying to God asking for forgiveness. It says it in the Word, Jesus said all you have to do is *"believe with your heart"*. You may slip up along the way many times or maybe try to go back to drugs, sex, violence and gossip, but God never changes He loves us unconditionally, you can't fool God. You can't keep sinning wilfully.

Will I go to Heaven? That is the question, heaven must be one big place not just one floor where you bump into everyone and anyone. God said there are rewards in heaven, and many mansions. How many times has God instructed us about his law and commandments? I believe if you are faithful to the best of your ability you will be in for a big surprise at the rewards in heaven.

Someone that is about to die who was a criminal, a killer or evil person and they sincerely gave their life to Jesus will go to heaven. There are many mansions (departments) in heaven, you can reach heaven *'JUST BECAUSE'* you believe in God with all your heart and love Him!

Romans chapter 10 verse 9.

Listen carefully mate, not everyone gets a last breath to give his or her life to God! I reckon if you loved God but didn't fully follow the instructions and commandments, you won't have much of a reward in heaven because you may not have told people about Jesus much or love much, God still loves us but, would you rather barely make it into heaven, cleaning the beautiful place in heaven or fellowshipping with all the great peeps like Jesus, Moses, Abraham, John, David and all the great people who made it into Heaven and "asking them questions seeing what's popping! Heaven must be the boom I imagine being able to fly there, sing all day, worship, praise, dance, and relax.

"NOTHING CAN COMPARE TO WHAT IT IS GOING TO BE LIKE IN HEAVEN!

Over-understanding! The devil like's to toy and tell you, no it's boring, church is boring, no need to pray and no need to repent.

See what I'm saying about understanding, God says his people are destroyed by lack of knowledge, which is people in general *"SOCIETY"* not just Christ like people.

God is talking about everyone, people are easily drawn to the lusts of the world and get caught up in the temporary things in this world.

Work *9 – 5,* meeting different people, sleeping with this one, that one, getting drunk, going clubbing every weekend.

This is societies (world) view of enjoying life, people get lost in these things! God is saying seek Him and be aware of Him, worship Him, do good works, love, spread the good news. God loves everyone and He wants you to come to paradise, heaven.

"Check this out Proverbs Chapter 29 Verse18.

What is it gonna be, are you gonna worship the devil or the Lord.

The devil is patient he we will wait for years days, to take you out! Do you remember when the devil was trying to play with Jesus's mind (God as Man) and asked Him to turn the stone into bread or jump off the cliff so the angels can catch him and all that jazz!

Jesus just quoted the devil *THE WORD,* "Man shall not live by bread alone but by the *WORD OF GOD!*

" What a silencer".

Circumstances and issues ain't always the devil's fault, look at life this way, God has predestined your future. *'Understanding',* your life can't be predestined in the will of God, if you do not live for Him.

If you are in Christ, by accepting Him and living for Him, your life will be predestined for good. Although the life of sin and evil you used to live, will be forgotten, meaning your old nature and past sins won't be held against you. Coz God meets you were you're at and turns all the bad things in the past for your good and His glory. You then become a new creation, old things are passed away and everything becomes new.

Pride

Over-understanding! One would ask questions about how does this guy know if the devil is real, heaven, hell, how to live, what is righteous, what is not.

It's simple you have just got tap into the supernatural and spiritual world, how do you do that? Read the Word (The Bible) to get to know God's character, have a relationship with Him and then your spiritual eyes gets more and more sophisticated!

"Bro, God is REAL AND LIVE! Like a live wire!

I remember when I had to swallow my pride one season, and signed on for benefits, coz I had no job or income coming in.

I could have exercised my faith, but I was not really at that level I should have been spiritually then. I was new in my Christian walk and did not have the know-how to effectively tap in. But as I grew spiritually in the knowledge, righteousness and the things of God, I made a decision to never ever claim benefits or sign on again!

Now I am here with my own computer *Monday 28ᵗʰ April 2003* writing my book with a job to go to tomorrow.

Someone that has not had a job for weeks on end, and is waiting for a desirable job that has not come through yet, needs to swallow their pride and *sign on for some benefits*. Until they get that job, or get up off their behind and find any job to do in the meantime, instead of making excuses, I used to make excuses for a long time.

One thing I always say to people is don't do anything, have value in yourself. You may not know what you would like to do long term but you should have an Idea of what you like to do or what you would like to do. Coz if you don't, you will just take anything that comes your way and may not be happy in the job/career long term, if you decide to do anything. However, sometimes, a man needs to do, what a man needs to do for a while, just a while.

You may need to do any type of legitimate work/job to get by, make a living and pay your bills. But make sure you HABAKKUK 2:2 IT, set yourself a goal, and a time period. Next ACTION, act by actively looking for what you like to do or what you would like to do long term as a job/career, as you are currently earning, with the frame of mind that you're pressing towards your long term goals.

When I mentor people, I always say we are all on a mission individually, and we must complete our mission, the only person that can complete our mission is us. Me, you, nobody else can. If you don't set out to complete your mission in life, no one will, if you don't work hard you won't get.

Some people are just too proud to put their hand to the plough, you must be prepared to work for what you want in this life, your dreams and success won't just fall on your lap, people perish when they have no vision, so activate your VISION.

Over-understanding! *"Wisdom"*. Giving is like giving shares in a good shares company it definitely comes back to you. God says He loves a cheerful giver, what you sow is what you reap, if anyone ask anything of you, if you have it give it. That is the God kind of Love the Lord wants to see.

True 'worship' focuses on God's Holiness, so forget pride and worship Jesus. Read these powerful chapters below.

Proverbs chapter 13 verse 10 (Pride) Proverbs chapter 16 verse 18 (Pride) Proverbs chapter 29 verse 23 (Pride) 1 Timothy chapter 3 verse 6 (Pride).

The reason why God loves a cheerful giver is coz it's an act of worship, love, serving, and it displays His character. In a church it builds unity, there is power in unity, like for instance who pays for the building we all worship in? Someone has to nothing is free!

Why shouldn't God be jealous? He is jealous in a caring, protective, compassionate, concerned, and loving way! After all He died for you and me so we may have life, or He could have left it that way and not come and it would have been harder for anyone to get to heaven, probably almost impossible.

God had to come down to earth and suffer pain as a man, as a sacrifice of *"SIN"* so He desires us all to come to Him, why wouldn't He be jealous. God's Word is Yes and Amen?

God takes pride in giving to us!

It's awesome how I can talk about some topics I haven't understood in the past but now I do for instance God calls us friends, God has chosen us, if we are gonna go *"through,* or God is putting us *"through,* we need to realise all the weapons we have and be on our guard.

Use these weapons to resist the devil, our shield, sword gun, and bazooka: 'The Bible', and 'The Word' (God's Mind).

Speaking the power, the Word "In Faith!

The devil would like you to bow down and worship him, so if you're deep in sin he will use it to push you further into it. He will eventually make you feel you have got totally lost and don't have a heart or willingness.

He will make false promises that seem to be harmless, pretending to offer you everything, or offer you money, sex, drugs, false love, any material things!

Call the devil's bluff, tell him where to go and to get lost!

The devil's pride never pays off.

Wisdom

Over-understanding! The wisdom of God caused me to write a book, God's wisdom caused me to look in a dictionary, and to look in the concordances.

People are watching you on a day-to-day basis you might be that good example God wants to use, to deliver someone, to be an encouragement and help the lost to understand more about Him. Working out certain things is just applying wisdom. Where does that true wisdom come from? *"You are correct again my friend"*, God. We need to recognise we can have it. You probably can fly in heaven you know? You must be able to coz we are gonna have a different body, similar to that Neo guy in the Matrix film.

How do we know what Heaven looks like? How are we reassured? I'm telling you man the Bible (God's Mind) is deep coz its all God wants us to know! Just have faith.

Heaven is gonna be beautiful, eyes have not seen, how beautiful it is gonna be! He created us for Himself,

The more you *'seek God'* the more He gives you clues, and shows you what is gonna happen. As we can see from His mind He has used many people as examples to show them visions and glimpses of stuff why? Coz they seeked after God! So He showed them stuff, if we seek too we will see so many things that will in the natural *"blow your mind"* and take your breath away! The glory of God all mighty is available for everyone.

Just tap in Son! God's Voice Shakes Tha Earth! Man I'm reassured, but one of my prayers is to stop taking things and facts for granted!!

It's real son! 1 Corinthians chapter 3 verse 19: The world's (society's) wisdom is foolishness, it's plain to see! Wisdom is better than silver or Gold (Proverbs 16 verse 16) (Proverbs chapter 9 verse 10)

Proverbs chapter 1 verse 2 (Wisdom) Proverbs chapter 4 verse 5 (Wisdom)

James chapter 1 verse 5: If you lack Wisdom ask God for some and He will give it to you according to His will.

"What more do I need to say but to just simply seek God for yourself, and see the power, reality, presence and manifestation of God in your life!

God is real.

Make sure YOUR conscious is clear, not thinking about someone else's!

Traffic Lights

Over-understanding! Heaven is like traffic lights to me, I go past traffic lights, every day, sometimes I just get past, some times I jump it (when no one is around, naturally) some times I just have to stop and wait, which can get boring and irritating sometimes, coz I wanna go about my business. I just wanna go, you can wait, and wait at the stoplight, waiting for your turn, when the light turns green it's time to put your foot down and move, that day when I'm in heaven and the angel opens the book of life and says: "yeah *Teslim* good to see you, your name was written in this book of life in 1999 come on in! I will be smiling and running in, diving in headfirst!

Will you be there and stay on the red light forever or will the light turn green for you and the angel tells you to come on in? Or will you just miss the green light?

Faith!

Over-understanding! I don't even know how to spell the majority of the words I have spelt in this book, thank God for technology though it can help. I had to keep spell checking words, that's the wisdom of God, the level you can be taken to when you let the Holy Spirit take control, pressing into the faith, and being willing to be guided is overwhelming.

I used to say why do things always seem to be repeated in the Bible? (God's Mind) I now believe the reason is because they are true and it has to be repeated so that you get the drift and the point!

So it is soaks into your spirit and it can be used as a powerful tool.

Why are there different versions of the Bible? Why shouldn't there be, if something is true and right why not share and break it down for everybody. Don't miss the point partner, I find mainly the Muslim guys I have spoken to whilst evangelising say there are different versions of the Bible (God's Mind) as if there were all different stories.

That's why I keep emphasising on analysing, the Bible (God's Mind), there is a reason for a lot of versions of the Bible (God's Mind) it is to make the Word easier to understand.

In this day and age I believe that a lot of men and women were led to break down the Bible in an easier reading format, some people don't want to move with the time.

I am not an English scholar. I prefer the real deal, the King James translated Version or amplified there are loads of other ones. New translation is fine although it's ideal to have the original as well as other translated Bibles (God's Mind).

Now the Mormon bible, that's a completely different something! It's like an (OTT) version, *yeah "over the top version"* of irrelevant stories, they are dealing with their own doctrines. The Mormons need to be constantly challenged and asked if they understand the Bible (God's Mind) fully yet, and the covenants and lessons! It's all about Jesus and nobody else! No one knows the Bible (God's Mind) fully. It's fresh all the time it is read, *"Alright then"*. I love the guys but they are causing danger and confusion, coz they don't make sense. Check out a good book talking about this cult religion Mormonism by John Ankerberg & John Weldon The Facts On The Mormon Church. They can do the explaining more justice than I can.

Hebrews chapter 10 verse 38 (**Faith**) Hebrews chapter 11 verse 1 (**Faith**) **James chapter 2 verse 20**: Faith without works is dead, faith without 'action' my friend is useless. You need to activate your faith with 'action' by God's Word. Take authority by guidance from the Holy Spirit. Jesus is the only wise God: 1 Timothy chapter 1 verse 17....

Relationship

I have such a relationship with God you now, He makes me laugh, and I know I must definitely make Him laugh.

DON'T TRY TO PLEASE MAN BUT JESUS CHRIST.

Do you identify: *"It has to be personal to you that JESUS died for YOU!*

What skills do you posses, whatever it is God will use you as you are, just be willing!

It's appalling some Christians, don't even know what **Amen** or **Hallelujah** means, and this term is used in church more than a million times, *I'll tell ya anyway.* **Amen** means (so be it) or in another occasion (It is so), and **Hallelujah** a 'Hebrew' word that means (Praise God) and can be said: '**Highest Praise**' this word came from the 'Hebrew' word for 'praise' 'Hallal' meaning (extreme praise). **Alleluia** is the same word, but the 'Greek' term!

Not picking on every Christian (Christ like people) but some have been around for years and don't study to show themselves approved or have a revelation.

They wait till Sunday to get it from the pastor

"I hope you're convicted bro!

Over-understanding the things of God, parables, proverbs, basics, do you understand it? *"Find out",* I would rather do what God says in the Bible (God's Mind) and wait for God's spontaneous blessings or revelation instead of waiting to hear it from a preacher all the time, "Aye", behave yourself, don't get it twisted now coz there is a difference in waiting and seeking, coz we all know faith cometh by hearing, hearing by the Word of God, but Christians can be lazy *"okay I put my hands up!*

How do I (Teslim) pray: "Your prayer doesn't have to be always long, it's about communication and relationship.

You can pick any chapter or scripture in the Bible (God's Mind) and vibe off that something like

READ: Psalms Chapter 23.

My typical prayer would sound something like this: *May the meditation of my heart and the words of my mouth be acceptable to you, Lord give me Your beauty for my ashes, let your people see your grace so they can be able to abide under your shadow, Lord forgive me for switching today, have your way in me, use me for your glory Holy Spirit fall afresh on me.*

Then I may go into worshipping by singing a love song to God, then praying for several people and being led by the Spirit. See not that long is it!

Pin Number To Heaven

Over-understanding! If you do not know Jesus Christ that died for your sin, God as Man you need to know Him!

Tomorrow might be too late. Nobody knows what tomorrow holds, I certainly don't, but I know what I would wanna be doing for tomorrow and I have faith I will be around tomorrow.

You need God now, tomorrow ain't guaranteed friend, to no one! I, Teslim took one minute out to give my life and allowed God's presence to come into my life.

We all get to the point of knowledge and understanding that the world is not enough.

Why are you created? Is it just to drink yourself silly, have sex, smoke drugs, and faff around?

There is more to life than this corrupted world, what goes around comes around, what you make happen for other people, will happen to you.

God helps those that help themselves, many are called few are chosen, you are chosen if you want to be chosen! By accepting God's promises and by carrying out the will of God, by making yourself available to be chosen!

When I was set free, I broke down crying, realising I had found peace, like that peace is Heaven, tears of freedom rolled down my face!

Friend this world is a dangerous and evil world, people don't seem to care anymore and the system doesn't seem to give a damn sometimes. You can't give up you have to go out there and take it by force! Take what? Take your peace, your ambitions, your dreams, your visions, your integrity, and your focus and love others!!

YOU LIVE ONCE AND DIE ONCE!

Over-understanding!

God forgave me all the times I lied

God forgave me all the times I beat people up

God forgave me all the times I stole

God forgave me all the times I had immoral sex

God forgave me all the times I was angry

God forgave me all the times I messed up

God forgave me all the times I cussed

God forgave me all the times I didn't listen to Him

He will not forgive you if you do not come to a place of repentance!

He will forgive you if you come to a place of repentance and regret!

God resists the *proud,* and gives *grace* to the *humble, Wow!*

Lean not on you own Understanding, but acknowledge God.

198

Steps To Overstanding Him!

1. Get an easy combined Bible (God's Mind) with King James and Amplified or an easy version, even a kid's Bible. I like books with pictures in it, I find it easier *it helps you know,* with scriptures and chapters, which you can understand and get a revelation from. I have about four different Bibles including a kiddie one, I love pictures and I'm 24 years old it's all good, it's about what you can identify with!

2. Get a Bible Commentary, a Bible Concordance or a Bible (God's Mind) with a concordance in it, that breaks down the Bible (God's Mind), and answers.

3. Study with excitement

4. Get some good tapes and music videos YOU enjoy, there are loads of different gospel music, Rap, Rock, Pop, Jazz, Soul, Reggae, loads of variety. Look on the Internet, or go into your local gospel and Christian shops and churches.

Once saved always saved?

Over-understanding! Are you a real Christian?

Can you lose your salvation?

Galatians chapter 5 verse 22 states the fruit of the Spirit.

Ephesians chapter 5 verse 3 4 5 states people who practice these types of sins will not enter Heaven.

Also according to Mark chapter 3 verse 28 – 29. If you are really a Christian you will walk in the fruits of the Spirit, if you do not demonstrate any traits of the fruits of the Spirit you are not really saved.

I can say this coz John chapter 7 verse 24 says to judge with a righteous judgement read: John chapter 15

YOU MUST BEAR FRUIT.

On this note when I'm at work I go onto this website (www.bible.com)

Release It!

Over-understanding! God can actually use you, when you give Him full access to your life, and your issues by letting Him take away and destroy everything He needs and wants to, to use you. There is no use holding crap tight, in your hand, if I were God I would be fed up and leave you until you feel like submitting fully to my will, but the deep thing is God never gets fed up.

I wouldn't want God to pass me by and wait for Him to come round again, that's long. I would take the chance straight away!

Brothers and sisters I can truly testify and say God kept me when the church I attended hurt me and my best friend Damian died at the same time, my life was hard I went through depression! *"Can you identify?*

Giving your life a thousand times, what is really the point? You only need to do it once. At the same time there must be a breaking point where you start picking up the basics of Christ!
A point where you get bored, having to give your life to be born again a thousand times. Being born again, how many times do you want to be born again?

I came to a point where I was just fed up of repeating myself it was like come on Teslim you are playing yourself grow up and rise up and make a choice to follow Christ and live right.

It's similar to the catholic method going up to the confession box a million times God heard you the first time! In another sense it's a good service to have! Coz you're releasing your guilt! But the Bible tells us to cast our burdens on to Jesus so let us confess to Him and release all.

Society can't actually believe and understand that the truth is right here, right now, available to everyone. The truth of God that you need, the truth to get you into Heaven!

This truth is in that Holy Bible (God's Mind) but people don't think it can be that easy. It is, everything is in the Word (The Bible)

REALISE GOD IS GOD, He created everything, what a creator and artist we all have different fingerprints, thoughts, moods, skills, bodies, tastes and God's gifts, God also designed many animals and insects wow.

I remember one time in my early Christian walk I came to the point in my life that I had to stop and re-examine my belief and walk with God, I asked Him a lot of personal questions and received answers.

Total confidence in God, dancing for God, is a must, that is where the breakthrough comes coz you are demonstrating faith! God loves it!

To the person reading this book, I wanna say: "Hi", "I don't know you", "but I care about you", and I want you to be successful and go to Heaven. I wanna also let you know God knows you, and He knows everything about you, and everything you are going through.

God can set you free trust me! My life is an example it is actually surprisingly true the Bible (God's Mind) is a right way of living! *The way of life,* man can't comprehend and believe, the truth that it is that close the right way of life is within reach. The way is here! Can you still be a nice person if you are not Christian? Of course you can. You can still be righteous of course, but you will not inherit heaven! You can choose the world's way (society) of living or God's way.

My friend Eddie Tettey said: *"You can drag a horse to the water but you can't make the horse drink it! I can give you the key but I can't make you use it!*

Over-understanding! You die once and once only!

What are you doing behind closed doors? Why don't you bring the burden you have to God.

"Spoiling the fun, or joining the fun? You need to break out of sin my friend, sin can be all so sweet but we need to break out of sin and reject sin!

I did it, so can you. I believe in you friend God believes in you too!!

The *Spirit is talking here so you better take heed!* None of the twelve disciples took any luggage with them when they joined Jesus. They were cool throughout their entire journey, following Jesus Christ, that's what a person does when they decide to carry their cross and follow Jesus Christ! Surrender everything!

When you surrender God gives you authority and power in Him, He gives you the ability to do all things in His name! We all have had a lot of pain stored up and people may still have pain stored up but we need to release it. The way I did it was by worship, which has become a strong point, when I'm communicating to God I release my pain and hurt through crying and praying, I recommend crying, praying and laughing they are good remedies coz when you use them you get delivered from stuff!

Over-understanding, the key to everything you are looking for is in 'SEEKING' 'FIRST' THE 'KINGDOM OF GOD' AND 'HIS' 'RIGHTEOUSNESS', that is, all 'His' 'Righteousness' and then watch how everything falls into place as you do this.

Read Matthew chapter 6 verses 33, Jesus is talking here! This is actually the key to success in 'Life' and with 'God'. Understanding not to seek God last but seeking Him 'first' in everything you do.

In the book of Matthew chapter 26 verse 41 Jesus is speaking again, instructing us all to consistently watch and pray, so that we do not fall into temptation. Temptation is always waiting and knocking at the door. But Jesus assures us that the <u>Spirit</u> (Holy Spirit) <u>indeed</u> (in action) is <u>willing</u>, but the flesh (carnal/mortal body) is weak. So we need to be led by the Holy Spirit of God. To watch, observe be cautious, sober and pray!

Music Creates An Atmosphere!

Over-understanding! Think about it, how do you react when you hear certain music? The music you listen to creates certain atmospheres, and feelings, even memories!

I said earlier when I used to listen to DMX, Flip mode squad and Eminem it made me feel a way.

I either wanted to get on rowdy and 'bruk wild' coz they used to relate to me and the life I was living at the time, so it always seemed to justify what I was doing, but the fact of the matter is, it's wrong.

We don't wanna go backwards we need to move forward, the majority of the music that is out there these days, contain swear and cuss words. They talk about killing a nigger, killing people, racism, hate, revenge, getting paper, what's that gonna do for the new generation? Your right again nothing! It promotes violence, drugs, immoral sex, anger, guns, jealousy, envy, greed, crime and non-unity.

A few of the smooth grooves, soul, funk music promotes lust, sleeping around, and talks about sex and intimacy between male and females in a explicit manner, it doesn't edify (BENEFIT), improve, or teach nobody. Does it. Cool your fine if your going to a party and it's for a good cause, a christening, wedding, birthday, but you if you are going clubbing and feel you know you are gonna be tempted to do certain things, you constantly have to search yourself, your motives and your heart. *Obviously we live in this world, and it is a challenge already but there has to be a "BALANCE".*

Music you listen to, company you keep, bars, parties, restaurants you attend, God has to outweigh the "Balance" weighing down anything else! Fun is always there to have and enjoy but don't let silly mix ups delay your blessing. Seek Him and you will find Him. Don't Procrastinate. *Stop delaying!* It's not some people that drift away, or have lack of strength and weaknesses we all face them. **Music is a powerful medium.**

We forget sometimes Greater is He that is in you than he that is in the world when you are a Christ follower. *"So who's bearing the fruit of the spirit then?*

"Hey I heard DMX (formerly Known as Dark man X) is turning Christian wow that's deep!

And to think I used to idolise this rapper!

Ma$e the rapper gave up counterfeit peace for the real thing too, he is a true Christian now, and Cliff Richard, Bonno from the big rock band U2, Mary J. Blige, Lauren Hill, MC Hammer!

I could go on about all these big stars. Celebrities and famous people are clocking onto Jesus. Have a look in most of the rappers and singers albums these days they mention Jesus Christ and acknowledge Him, most of the stars are not living the life or perfect but they have at least started! *You see Jesus will work for everyone!*

Bad music can influence your actions and pollute your mind.

You can get good positive music, tapes and Cd's that will renew your mind and edify (Benefit) and also minister to your spirit, there is different gospel music, Rap, Rock, Pop, Jazz, Soul, Reggae, loads of variety. Look on the Internet, or go into your local gospel and Christian shops and churches.

Bad music can influence your actions and pollute your mind.

Over-understanding we were created to worship God

Get that revelation imbedded in your mind that the devil is harmless because Jesus lives in us! Satan who was named Lucifer, by God, which means "son of the morning" was the most beautiful angel created, and the man in charge of music, so don't be surprised by Satan's skills, and how music is today because it has been corrupted a great deal today and influenced by the devil (The mischievous one).

POSTIVE

Who gave you a label?

Was it the negative 2pac, 50 pence/5o cents, wu tang,

p diddy, SONY or death row?

Who branded your area or community a bad label?

All these negative talking these rappers promote is fables!

Righteous role models need to influence on the get go!

So let's get together encouraging and say so!

We need to put the truth on the table!

Let's get the positive vibes routed like a cable?

Investment in negative vibes can be fatal!

Gun crime and crime is a low joke show!

So let's get together in unity change things for the GOOD and let right
vibes flow!

Proverbs chapter 1 (Wisdom)

Proverbs chapter 4 verse 23 guard your heart

Psalms chapter 100

Maintain!

Over-understanding! How does one maintain being a Christian? To maintain is simply by constant prayer, constant worship to God The Father.

Ask God: *"create in me a clean heart"*.

Remind yourself *"Greater is He in me than he that is in the world.*

Tell God *"may the words of my mouth and the mediation of my heart be acceptable to you. Focus!*

"I ask you again can you identify with long suffering I mean looooooooooooooooooong suffering. We always have to go through the testing. We need to grow and bear fruit, bear means we can *tolerate* we can *stand and grow in spiritual maturity and character.* Fruit means we can *outgrow and produce,* the more life becomes a challenge it gets easy coz we identify with peeeeeeeeeeeace!

Sometimes you may not feel like loving or being righteous, but it's about making a conscious choice no matter what.

If you find you are struggling then put some gospel worship music on to renew your mind. Our minds need constant renewing. Also lean not onto your own understanding, call a friend, or someone you can talk to, you can even call a prayer line. It is important you pray no matter how short it is even if you just say Holy Spirit help me, or Lord Jesus help me.

Have faith knowing God will never leave you or forsake you.

"I'm a regular guy, just like anyone else, flesh and blood, a sinner, saved by grace.

Proverbs chapter 13 verse 20: He that walks with wise company shall be wise.

Corinthians chapter 15 verse 33: Bad company corrupt good morals

Overstanding! Focus, *vision, confidence authority over circumstances, integrity with faith!* We have to *"ride it"* we are all equal.

1 John Chapter 2 Verse 27: We all have the same anointing.

Don't give up dreaming, coz when you give up dreaming you end up with no vision or like a tramp, drug addict, or alcoholic trying to escape reality.

Cussing ain't right, we all do it at times, I know we go through tuff times and feel like belching out combos of cuss words but it's not good to cuss. You should not swear and cuss!

Just like the ten commandants is a foundation of morals to follow. Lets follow a life style of edification, learning from one another, being accountable to each other putting each other in check! We are all Jesus's disciples and we are all God's sons and daughters!

Read: Ephesians chapter 4 verse 29

*God has made one blood and one spirit, simply check out His mind in this scripture in **Acts** chapter 17 verse 26-28 God has the ability to slide through the Word (God's Mind) displaying His glory and will.*

As I said before in this book if you have one of those excuses I used to have bout not understanding The Bible, buy a good translation or one that breaks things down to you for easy reading. "That's understanding! There are so many translations out there that can help you, what are you doing to be Christ like?

What would God say?

Overstanding! Hygiene, wash your mouth, your teeth, your skin, look after yourself its wisdom the same with our insides.

Be sober, the clubs you attend, films you watch, the balance, the balance, the balance sort out the balance. You must balance. The righteous path, God's Word and commandments have to out weigh these cares of the world!

"The devil is the player" *"God is the games master"...*

Overstanding!

Fact *Jesus was sinless He did not descend from Adam*

Fact Jesus was the only one born by a virgin birth

Fact *Jesus walked on water (On the Sea to be exact)*

Fact Jesus rose again from the dead, He actually came back to life when He died!

Fact *Jesus is coming back again!*

Fact Jesus lived the lifestyle as man! But He was God in the flesh

Fact *Jesus did miracles*

Fact Jesus fulfilled Scripture prophecies

Fact *Jesus died for our sins by shedding His blood.*

There is a Jesus, Joshua the Hebrew name that means salvation, salvation is now known to be Jesus,

JESUS IS THE SALVATION! *Jesus fulfilled His coming He fulfilled scripture a million times over!*

There are so many ways to say His name, Jesus, Zeus, Iesus, Jesu, Jah, Yahweh, Jehovah, His Word is **Yes** and **Amen,** He is life!

God (Jesus) became poor to make us rich!

Please do your own research! He has many, many more names check it out.

Chapter 23

It's All Spirits

Take the situation and speak to it! *We have to speak life always,* life is 'positive words' 'righteous words' 'living words' speaking into existence, and casting down imaginations. Imaginations are thoughts, the negative thoughts and imaginations.

We get loads of thoughts day in day out, so cast down those hindering and distracting thoughts!

'Pull Down' strong holds, with your authority: The Word of God concerning what Jesus has giving us authority to say!

We need to constantly walk in the Spirit and be led by the Sprit.

"Told you before" God hides nothing, He gives you the wisdom to find out what certain stuff, parables, proverbs, riddles, stories, lesson and words mean, God is good we either get led by the Holy Spirit of God or not.

<u>Read: Ephesians Chapter 1-</u>

Read the whole of Romans chapter 8, 1 John Chapter 2 Verse 27

Get out of the bad habits, get out of the rowdy vibes, ask the Holy Spirit to help you and guide you, He will! What do you think He is there for?

The Holy Spirit is a Spirit, which is *righteous, saintly, **sanctified**, divine, **heavenly**, virtuous, **moral**, worthy, powerful, **honest**, honourable, **perfect**, good, **of God**, of Love!*

I remember one incident that happened, when the spirit of anger and violence came upon me in my early Christian walk and I did not know how to deal with it at the time.

I was on 'trying to be a good Christian tip' at the time, all of the time. I must have been waiting to get on a bus and a man ran past me he pushed me out of the way to get on the bus.

It triggered my anger. As I was getting on the bus I pushed him back and he pushed me again, then I left it, and told him to grow up and get out of my way so I could sit down. He wouldn't so I pushed him out of my way again then the man suddenly yanked my new gold chain off my neck which snapped into pieces on the floor it was my favourite chain.

I was so vex and surprised, I froze and stood there on the bus in anger, the anger was getting stronger, it dominated me as soon as the man got off his stop, I got off and moved to him, I dragged him to the floor and I stomped on this mans face and chest, then ran off before the police caught up to me.

I had actually thought I had changed back then in *2001*.

I surprised myself, I was still under construction my anger was due to my lack of walking in the 'Holy Spirit'.

<u>Read Ephesians Chapter 2-</u>

There's things you will say and want to do coz of how you feel at the time. At times the Holy Spirit directs us to do something else, this is where some people misunderstand Christians.

You say I will do this, or if you're angry I will do that, but coz we are led by the Holy Spirit we might not actually do what we said. The Holy Spirit could lead us to do something completely different.

You need to keep hearing the Word, which is the power we need to be ready to battle all times against the demonic spirits. *THE HOLY SPIRIT HUMBLES'...*

The devil has power on the earth, but not over you unless you let him walk all over you.

How does he gain access? "I'll tell you, little by little, he will tempt you, then walk all over you.

When you let God into your life you don't change straight away it is a process, like a seed planted. God helps you and the Holy Spirit in you becomes active more and more advanced and you become more sensitive!

Righteousness kicks in, the spirit of violence, anger, sex, lust masturbation (sexual immorality), depression and crime gets broken into pieces.

<u>Read Ephesians Chapter 3-</u>

Spirit of drugs, throw the drug, spliff to the floor and get high on Jesus!

WISDOM & TRUTH! Don't get caught in mix up. Like is Jesus really His name? Did He die at the age, month or exact time everyone says he did? Did he have brown hair, black hair? Was it a wooden cross he died on? People will keep asking questions till Jesus comes back. God's son's name is Jesus and at the name of Jesus every knee has to bow, there is power in His name, so it must be real!

When He comes back if you have died you will be in heaven with Him. If you are still here you will witness something heavy and fantastic!

God says you will disappear into heaven so it will be like that film 'Back To The Future' when that guy disappears, you will disappear into heaven paradise to be with God. That is the **RAPTURE**, you can read about it in the book of <u>1 Corinthians chapter 15</u>, <u>1 Thessalonians chapter 5</u>, and **Revelations** in the Bible. There is a spiritual supernatural kingdom, all you have to do is tap in to it, open your spiritual eyes.

Spirit of anger, hate, worry, jealousy, depression, greed, and lust needs to be abandoned today!

There are tons of spirits in the atmosphere there are good (righteous spirits) and bad (evil spirits).

I believe we all have a common knowledge of when someone has a good spirit or a bad spirit you can feel it. Whether you fully activate your spiritual eyes is a different thing!

The supernatural realm is noticed when your spiritual mind and eyes are activated, then you can be spiritually conscious at all times and you can see what is popping and taking place physically and also in spiritual (supernatural) realm.

"Quite therapeutic! *It's all Sprits!*

I'm gonna deal with the spirit of homosexuality, now hear my heart, homosexuality is a choice!

I'll explain with guidance from the Holy Spirit as I said before earlier we all have a choice and when we decide to do something or submit to our choice there is nothing anyone can do, not even God!

We all have the opportunity to try out unusual things and as human beings we are curious, curious of what it may feel like to change normality, by that I mean changing the normal and moral and set foundation.

I do not feel anybody is born homosexual, but from a young age this is where it is vital parents take responsibility.

I feel this responsibility has been neglected and some parents have not had the chance or choice to take responsibility so the child suffers, as different spirits lurk in the atmosphere a boy can feel a girl's tendencies and behave feminine or a girl can feel a boy's tendencies and behave masculine.

Parents have to train their children.

If it's a boy, well the mother and father would develop the boy and teach and train the boy to be a man, and if it's a girl the mother and father would develop the girl and teach and train the girl to be a woman.

So therefore I guess both parents have to take their place in their roles! It would be beneficial if the boy spends more time with the father and the girl spend more time with the mother, obviously as kids grow up they are influenced by the genders around them and discover the difference between 'male' and 'female'.

Besides that we can't see what is going on out of the house, such as what goes on in school, or in someone else's care, the only thing to do here is to always be alert, pray and have faith.

What am I trying to say here? Well simply after parents have taken their responsibility and their child grows to a young adult I am confident that their child is *'less likely'* to be a homosexual person, coz it's a choice, just like sleeping around it's all sin and sexual immorality!

Homosexuality is a unnatural spirit, the spirit of homosexuality is everywhere waiting to dominate us all. We either choose that way and accept it or choose what we have been given and put the functions into use the moral way!

God made us all without a mistake. Natural means, usual, normal, accepted, expected! All homosexuals choose to reverse their natural nature because they are comfortable or content that way, I feel what can cause this is if a male or female has been neglected, or come from a broken home, or lacking self confidence in their self or gender, or suffered from abuse, sexual abuse, shown a false or negative impression on life or not trained, taught or shown their role or a moral way to be and act or not told any indication of his/her purpose. The reality is if you are a man and have a penis, you need to accept it. And accept that you are a man!

Or if you are a woman and have breasts and a vagina you need to accept it! And accept that you are a woman! We all individually need to accept and take our roles and be content!

This is not the case these days, things have been blown out of proportion and gone wrong and there are a lot of men or women who don't want to take their roles, or are not comfortable, content or confident with their *'natural nature'* for one reason or another. They choose what they are confident and comfortable in, such as a man desiring another man sexually and acting like a woman and vice versa.

THIS IS WRONG!

It's an unnatural spirit! I won't dwell on this subject for long but it's an issue, which needs to be addressed and clarified over and over again to stop the confusion!!! As there is a common ground, men need women and woman need men they are made for each other.

Every man, woman, boy and girl are precious and valuable in the sight of God and all have a purpose!!!

Please take control of your sexuality and do not be dominated by the homosexuality spirit.

Don't let it rule you and convince you that you are homosexual, or tell you that you are a man in a woman's body or vice versa "don't believe the hype it's a big lie from the pit of hell, it is not true, do not be fooled by that spirit or people who say it is normal!!!

It is not natural, I believe there is nothing wrong with men behaving more feminine than a regular man as long as he knows his place and role as a man and vice verse for women, but one shouldn't get it twisted. Just coz a man behaves more feminine he should not automatically be rejected as a man and labelled as a chi chi man, a batty man, or homosexual. Or the same with women coz they act more masculine they should not automatically be labelled a dyke, freak or lesbian.

Stop letting society and the media decide your destiny, the society and media do have a lot of influence in our lives and play a major part in influencing and convincing us!

"The question is are you gonna sit down and let them run your life?" "Don't give them the satisfaction! "

God does not like the sin of homosexuality. It is wrong.

Many people who label themselves homosexuals have been delivered from that spirit in the past and in the present. It's immoral to like our own gender we are born to multiply, reproduce and worship God.

This is not a normal or natural act therefore it is wrong! Again this is a choice however, we can be delivered by prayer and fasting!

I have learnt not to condemn or look at homosexuals in a different way coz they are all children of God and from God. 'Sin' is sin! And 'choice is choice!'

It says in the Bible (God's Mind) train a child in the way *'he'* or *'she'* should go as I said earlier I feel many results of homosexuality and bisexuality is down to the lack of parents taking responsibility, not fully taking their place, by training and bringing up their kids. You need to have time for your kids!

When you bring a human being into this world it is your responsibility, therefore you are responsible for that child! As long as he or she is a youth (1-16yrs) you have a responsibility for your child until they are old enough to make their own decisions!

Once your child is old enough to make their own decisions, continue to pray, if your child chooses to get caught up in the wrong association or relationship you can still pray, if you are very concerned about your child then fast and pray.

When someone is an adult they choose what they want to do and the fact is we all have a free will and a choice!

Another result I feel about homosexuality being wide spread, apart from choice, it is due to the *'power of association'*. Homosexuals associating with more homosexuals just cultivates and hides the lie, now I feel it would be wrong in saying we shouldn't mix with homosexuals or avoid them coz that would not be Christ like, as Jesus mixed with everyone. Otherwise how are we gonna get the good news across and salvation if we don't, but the idea is not to get involved in the acts they do such as sexual immorality or condoning their act!

You can encourage homosexuals with the love of Jesus Christ. As I was saying about responsibility I feel these situations have contributed by the influence of the spirit of homosexuality. Situations such as both parents not being around, the television, media, society, government, foster children, being brought up in a boarding school, sexual abuse the list goes on and on. *HOMOSEXUALITY IS A SPIRIT OF PERVERSION*

YOU CAN BE SET FREE FROM HOMOSEXUALITY!!!

Leviticus chapter 18 verse 22, **1 Corinthians** chapter 6 verse 9, 10, Romans chapter 1 verse 25-32, **Romans** chapter 8

In the Bible God's mind it says teach or train a child the way that he or she should go and when he or she grows he or she will not depart!

Not depart from what?

Not depart from the moral, right, fruitful foundations and self-discipline taught, and not being easily lead astray.

If you teach a young child the way he or she should go nine times out of ten they will keep on the straight and narrow path! And will not depart into immorality or bad things. **Proverbs** chapter 22 verse 6

<u>Read Ephesians Chapter 4</u>

Power In Association, Compromise, Temptations and Traps This Is Personal...

Don't compromise. The Holy Spirit ain't anything but righteousness! Don't do what society or the world does, which is waste their life away in clubs, getting drunk, sleeping around passing time etcetera, etcetera, etcetera.

I had a friend come to visit me one time that I hadn't seen in ages he just turned up, not at my front door. He waltz's in and saw my computer on, with notes all over my room and bits of paper and stuff so he thought he would be inquisitive which he was, you know, nosey, and asked me what was I getting up to?

I tried to avoid the question that was coming up but I couldn't coz at the time I was training myself not to lie, even in the smallest thing.

He asked me what I was doing so I just told him I was writing a book he started laughing, one of the things he said was why don't I write a book when I'm famous and well known by the media, in other words when I get my big break as an actor. Then I could sell my book more easily, he started making me think, and then I just had to suddenly repent in my mind and shouted at him saying this book is not about money it's about reaching out and encouraging the lost. *I don't give a damn about making money that was not the purpose of the book,* then he tried to have a debate, I immediately shut up, and changed the subject and asked him how his life was and what he has been up to, knowing suddenly in my spirit mind, I shouldn't be sharing certain things with him because some people try to make you lose focus.

A pastor I once knew always said be careful who you share your dreams or secrets with, and he would also say: *"guard your heart because out of it flows the issues of life"*, which is true.

Stop walking amongst the dead, the unfocused, the corrupter, and deceiver, the devil possessed people who are *"not for God"* who are *"against God"* it's easy to let demonic forces gain that access in your life!

God is the comforter. Sticks closer than a brother.

Don't be afraid to challenge people and tell them the truth, but sometimes you have to just shut up and let them learn wisdom for themselves the Holy Spirit does that!

No one is born perfect, but we can do the right thing, which is live, a righteous life!

Spiritual warfare 2 Corinthians Chapter 10 Verse 3 - 7

Just let the Holy Spirit guide you, the Holy Spirit of truth!

The weapons we have as Christians are mighty in the pulling down of strong holds.

Funny Christians

I used to think why are there so many funny Christians? (Christ Like People) Christians that claim to be Christians (Christ Like People) it clicked and hit home, it was lack of faith, lack of the Word, lack of prayer, lack of worship, lack of knowing God's character and mind, lack of integrity, lack of unity, and lack of love.

These things open the doorway to a judgemental spirit, spirit of bitterness, spirit of unforgiveness, spirit of guilt, spirit of jealousy. "See when your Holy Spirit seems to be asleep. This is coz we don't acknowledge it, coz we choke it with holding all these issues in our hearts so the discernment level drops, so you do silly things, you act like you don't care, your appearance changes, instead of looking and feeling like love the flesh does whatever.

"I call it flaky! Not trying to disrespect anyone, but this issue has to be addressed, coz it's true, remember the truth sets you free! People be shaking their head and agreeing, but it just goes to show there are many show boat Christians (Christ Like People) who put on the fake Christ like suit! Christians (Christ Like People) with no focus, no peace, lack of revelation, love, insecurity and faith!

That's what mashes up us Christians and causes us to have no unity! Faith without works is dead, lack of prayer causes 'talk no actions' it slows us Christians (Christ Like People) down! *"Be a go get it'*, let the love shine! *Lazy Christians wake up!*

Why do I have a right to say a lot of things and convicting stuff I say? Coz it's Holy Spirit inspired, the truth sets you free and coz I've been there, done it, worn the t-shirt and overcome it, now I can talk bout it!

We are like ants, God loves all and sees all, some perish, and some remain.........

Activate your FAITH...

Be led by the Spirit so we constantly walk in it!

Christians (Christ Like People) need to get to the level where you minister to yourself? Why coz the Holy Spirit (God) dwells in you!

Deal with your spirit mind. The Holy Spirit is Jesus, (God)

WHAT YOU LET IN IS WHAT YOU GIVE OUT

Matthew chapter 12 verse 34-35:

Luke chapter 6 verse 45: Out of the abundance of the heart the mouth speaks.

Proverbs chapter 5 verse 3: Guard your heart coz out of it flows the issues of life.

Ephesians Chapter 6 Verse 10 - 18

Chapter 24

Tapping In!

I kept avoiding reading the Word at one stage so I wouldn't be accountable for more knowledge, coz the more you read the more you get to know about God's character and His plans for your life, *the deeper the test the higher the call bro!*

There are so much ways to get God to listen to you and even your heart desires getting fulfilled. *"Shall I tell you? "Okay without further ado I'll tell you!*

JUST DO THE WORD! You just need to have faith and stand on His Word! You really think God likes you complaining all the time, you should be ashamed of yourself you Jesus nagger! I want this I want that?

Why on earth would God answer your particular prayer?

Faith Forgiveness Faith

Faith Belief

Submitting Your heart

Faith

Love

Faith

How much are you willing to grow?

Here's a pattern for you to follow!

1. How many people and lost souls are you helping

2. How willing are you

3. What is your agenda?

4. Fear him

5. Obey Him

6. Repent all times

7. Walk in Integrity and love

8. Declare what God says involving you, coz what God blesses no man can curse

9. Have Faith that is evidence, proof of what you cannot see, but it is there

"It's in God's spoken words about you! "Check it out!

Don't pray in vain!

Pray focused prayers with revelation and passion. Know whom you are praying to!

I can't forget where I came from!

Train your mindset, in the mindset of how God sees things! Be real and let this motto be established: *"it's all about love"*.

Keeping it tight!

Sometimes you just gots to sit there to let God and only God help you man,

GET CLEAN COME CLEAN BRO, stop trying to find different answers that don't make sense and confuse you, what your holding on today will be gone tomorrow, if you are trying to make a decision choose right!

Matthew Chapter 16 Verse 19

Hell is real, hell is deep, we all know demons are alive and breathing, they feed on sin. Sin weighs you down after a while.

You better be prepared for a change, things like friends changing on you when you decide to live for God, certain people won't like you anymore, people will tell lies on you by assassinating your character or try to bring your old self and past back by provoking you. Your mobile phone won't probably go off as much anymore boredom seems to kick in, basically you lose your so called friends. These are all the things I went through but you know what! Christians (Christ Like People) can have fun no more wasting your time in irrelevant things. When you start acting on things that's when it starts getting exciting. One of the key things is to follow the instruction God. Psalms Chapter 1 Verse 1

In the mornings and night times I pray repenting lots of times in fact all through the day every day. Things happen all through the day trying to knock you of course, people stepping on your feet, irritating you, giving you dirty looks, coughing behind and on you, swearing around you and all that jazz. "Just got to keep fighting that fight of righteousness bro, so none of these things gain access into your life and business, *"God's business, keep prayed up. In my early Christian walk* I had to stop the one-foot in one foot out nonsense, and come to the point where I wanted to be serious. And start all the way from the bottom again and work up to the top! *Are you fed up of sin yet? You need to be!*

Psalm Chapter 91 Verse 1

222

Chapter 25

What Is Your Ministry?

Bible talks about the five-fold ministry, which are:

1. Apostles messengers
2. Prophets inspire preachers
3. Evangelist who are preachers of the gospel travelling ministers, missionaries
4. Pastors the Shepherd of the flock the leader in the church
5. Teachers.

Ephesians 4v11

Sometimes I sit there and thank God for my anointing and talent, everyone has a talent and everyone has a good gift and talent that comes from God in heaven.

It's down to you if you activate it or not, we all have the same gifts available to us it's upto you tap in and be willing to activate it or not!

Read Ephesians chapter 1 verse 3

James chapter 1 verse 17 + Acts chapter 1 verse 8

I'll tell you how to acknowledge you ministry. Simply seek God, pray read about His love and walk in His love, open your heart to Him and let Him in, by coming to Him in spirit and truth always, repenting and releasing your cares to Him and reach and pull on Him.

When you really feel God's awesome presence you will cry like a baby with tears of joy. Forget the street knowledge, stop! Strive to live right get intoxicated with God's way and will for your life we are all created to walk in love, be unique and special!

It's all our duties to carry out the work of an evangelist! Spreading the good news of Christ the love, peace and joy the whole nine yards at home, work, with friends, family, on road on earth! This is our 'Core Ministry' we are all supposed to be evangelists spreading the gospel then as we act in this 'Core Ministry' we start to understand our purpose, our strength and our other ministries.

What is your ministry?

We all know what our ministry is now, we try to constantly avoid the high calling **Philippians Chapter 3 Verse 13 + 2 Timothy chapter 4 verse 5**

Matthew chapter 28 verse 19 + Mark chapter 16 verse 15

I tried to avoid it for ages but I couldn't anymore!

Now I get so excited when I'm at church praising God in spirit and truth coz He reveals so much to me in the mix of worshipping Him God can't help but to reveal mysteries to you and bless you when you FOCUS on His Holiness.

Your Ministry Of Love?

This is what it's all about "Love". There are people who need love whatever shape, size, form, colour, height, race, gender, age and background!

Agape Love, which means a God kind of love a friendly regardless love, **Phileo Love,** meaning a brotherly feeling and concentration kind of love, and a **Eros Love,** meaning a passion, sexual, arousal and fulfillment kind of love, a love demonstrated when you're married all these types of love including an **Eros Love** can be expressed to God in a sense of passion for God, gratification, arousal and fulfillment. In God is fullness of Joy! These are Greek words for love **Agape, Phileo, Eros.**

1 Corinthians Ch 13 / 1 Corinthians Ch 14

Matthew Chapter 5 Verse 44 *God says LOVE your enemies!*

The Five Fold Ministry: Apostles, Prophets, Evangelist, Pastors and Teachers.

What you see is what you get, there's a lot of reaching out to do, and it ain't gonna take just, north, south, east, west churches to do it we need to save souls and recruit more Christians, we need to be a sales man for Jesus Christ. I have found a lot of Christians these days are lazy some are in a comfort zone! You need to check yourselves and recognise and realise who you are in Christ!

We forget at times police, judges, musicians, actors famous people, people in power, are normal human beings just like you and me, its just a profession, they are all human beings that cry, lie, sin, we need to do our jobs properly as Christians, let us heal the broken hearted and save souls.

Life is a challenge meet it, life is a gift accept it, life is an adventure dare it!

HAVE VALUE IN PEOPLE.

Fulfil that promise and become that man or woman of destiny God has called us to be exposed, have a teachable spirit, stop stalling, and be man or woman of action!

It ain't easy to be a Christian the tools we need in this temporary world is money, maybe a car, a house, food but who created it? *"That's right God!* So He will have to provide which He will. I'm still shocked, amazed, flabbergasted, I'm saved! If you're lost and can't find yourself, check the friends you keep and the influences around you. Catch the vision go for Jesus and shine the light bright!

Stop avoiding the truth and being scared to make a commitment and make a fresh start!

I have learnt to hold things loosely, I realise nobody is perfect, everyone is different, he without sin cast the first stone!

I remember when I met the Queen of Jordan and spoke to her and shook her hand she did not get scared of my gold teeth or my dark skin. God will use you as you are! She seemed to sense a love about me and I sensed a love about her agape behaviour.

I feel I carry a presence everywhere I go. You will too!

Ask and it shall be given, coz it's already been given. God is God and He knows the beginning and end He wants us to pray in advance!

"Memorise scripture" the Word (The Holy Bible)

Don't miss the bus!

You have to keep your integrity

You have to keep loving

You have to keep focused, focused on God

You have to keep prayed up

You have to keep casting down imaginations

You have to keep pulling down strong holds

You have to keep seeking God

You have to keep fighting to be righteous

You have to keep standing on the Word the Bible

You have to keep worshiping, singing, thanking and praising God

You have to keep smiling and laughing

Trust me you will not be disappointed with Jesus!

226

When you know GOD for yourself, you can't be easily conned or false doctrinated! If you say: "Yeah I read this book but nothing has changed? Faith my friend, faith believe God, and it will, faith is the key. Without it you will not see the results manifest!

Your faith needs to be serviced and exercised daily! Get a revelation, you own that Greater thing inside of you! By seeking GOD Almighty!!!

If you don't step into your ministry you will never understand your purpose!

What You Become Is What You Do With The Promises, and Benefits Of God's Spoken Words And Gifts.

Philippians chapter 3 verse 12 - 15: Not that I know 'everything' about 'Christ Jesus', I just press towards the high calling in Christ Jesus in humility and passion knowing God's ways are past finding out, read: **Romans chapter 11 verse 33 – 36:** His ways are past finding out. He is the Almighty, the Alpha and the Omega, the beginning and the end, the Lilly of the valley, the bright and morning start, He is omnipotent, the only wise God: 1Timothy chapter 1 verse 17.

If you don't step into your ministry you will never understand your purpose!

What You Become Is What You Do With The Promises, and Benefits Of God's Spoken Words And Gifts.

Philippians chapter 4 verse 8: Finally Brethren, whatsoever things are true, whatsoever things are honest, whatsoever things are just, whatsoever things are pure, whatsoever things are lovely, whatsoever things are of good report, if there be any virtue, and if there be any praise, think on these things.

Chapter 26

Email To My Work Colleagues!

I copied and pasted this straight from the email I sent at work; so don't worry about tha spelling mistakes coz your getting the "actual 'real deal'.

Just an encouragement... God is real and he calls you and calls you, and when you only submit and recognise that call he shows himself strong! And reveal himself to you Why?To show you there is peace in him! I have been going through some big challenges in my life since this past 11 months spiritually, emotionally, mentally, phsically.

I remember sending out a mass email asking if anyone new a counselor and some people thought i was joking, gut goes to show, that we all individually go through tingz and at times it seems too much to bear and one feels like 'exploding'But God Knows all are cares and worries and he knows wot's poppoing.And actually wants you to take it to him.

I two years ago had a baaaaaaaaaaaaaaaaaad attitude! And did not give a damn I did anything and everything and did it to the maximum! I got fed up and realised there is more to life than certain things' I'm sure you all know wot i'm on about! Now I' am 24 I am wiser sometimes Old ways try to creep back in my life. But you know wot again LIFE is a challenge but we only have one shot at it!

There is definately a higher force God 'Jesus' and a deciving and evil force the 'devil'

In Jesus is the fullness of joy, in the devil is anger, destruction! I have been dealing with patients, faith, people and I have realised for the past 3 moths I have been trying to do a lot of things in my own strength and i have learn greater is he in me than he that is in the world! That great thing that is in me is God' tha world is temporary and we did not bring anything into this world when we came in and sure ain't gonna take nothing out when we leave it!

What am I saying?I am saying I have a peace a peeeeeeeeeeaaaaaaaaaacee though circumstances may try to hinder me and my faith and my life I have a focus!To get real peace not carnal/natural peace you need 'faith' Faith in God, patience and that is the real peace. God loves everyone and we can't live without God.I am thankful to be alive! We all are sinners and all can get peace.The peeeeeeeeeeeeeeeeeeaaaaaaaace of God Ain't far away my broda my sista. I ain't perfect and ain't gonna play i am coz every day is a constant battle and Challenge but I stand on the word, love and the peeeeeeeeeeeeeace of God! I'm letting tha light shine without loosing my identity! Phillipians chapter 4 verse 19˜

See wot it's saying at www.bible.comyou ain't got nothing to loose in reading this scripture in the bible God loves everyone and wants you to activate your spiritual eyes.

Peace! Agape..........Teslim Johnson

Chapter Twenty 27

A TESTIMONY

A testimony means: indication, witness, demonstration, statement, evidence and proof. "*Which this book is. My "Testimony! "I'm declaring something here!*

Well you've read it for yourself in black and white!

I took you through my life!

I took knocks and I had to ride it, and I struggled with issues I'm now over coming!

Get a grip bro! *You can't beat the system you always get caught!*

"I say a little prayer for you".

I remember different court cases being adjourned "bound in a three year cycle of paying court fines, criminal minded activities, trying to get out of crime, being put on probation, community service, petty and major stealing, getting caught. Over doing it going (OTT) by drinking, sex, fighting, loosing sense of reality wanting to be right.

"I must admit I sinned good, "from the age of nineteen I always used to say when I'm twenty five I wanna be rich or I will rob a bank! *I was serious!*

My life has done a 360 turn and I live a life of integrity and righteousness.

Remember I am not perfect!

The damage drugs did was making me forgetful, not having worries, red eyes, unconcerned, mood swings but God breathed afresh on me.

I used to make up excuses that I didn't see the scripture where it said couldn't swear or can't have sex or smoke weed I had no wisdom then. To think I was not aware that I used to battle with a drink problem for two years, and God has set me free.

Anytime I got vex I drank a can of Kestrel or Fosters extra strength beer, which was a quick drink of escaping reality that made me act very violent and cause me to black out. After one can of these beers I would be care free and completely drunk.

Where would I be if I was still in sin if I still kept in sin, if I had not changed? I would have definitely had a gun by now, coz the way the street is, it would seem to be a priority. I would have probably had a few unwanted kids, been on drugs or dead!

A lot of people and friends I know are either dead, on drugs, in jail or unhappy. God comes through for me all the time. He is never late He is always on time! He is there financially, emotionally, mentally, spiritually, externally and internally.

What do you do? How can you make a difference reaching out there? There's a dying world out there. Lets make a stand!!!

I watched a so-called man of God the Pastor of a church I trusted and used to attend fall deep into sin. The effect was I suffered from depression, I thought I would go crazy! I shaved all my hair off, anger choked my Christ likeness, my trust in people, Christians or any leader was gone, I was faithless but God resurrected me back again. I nearly lost God again but something in me could not give up. I went through hurt, anger, bitterness, depression, an eating disorder, I had a fiancée then I didn't have a fiancée.

Through it all I am still alive and kicking after being hurt somewhere I thought was the least place I would get hurt which was church. *God it hurt*. A lot of friends and fellow Christians suffered and I pray they are made whole right now in the name of Jesus.

I did not think I would trust again but I have gone through and carried my cross, it hurt but like a true soldier we go through the fire. In God we trust. God can still make you whole again, He is more than enough. He will never leave you or forsake you.

I know how it feels to be abused, hurt, betrayed!

A Wretch Like Me!

I had a fake driver's licence, now I have a clean one.

I used to drive on pavements? Yep I did that a lot, I'm not proud of it though!

I Had a bad bank account and bad credit now I have a steady bank account and good credit. I had loads of aliases not anymore, smoked drugs all night not no more, I beat up cab drivers not any more, I had no peace now I have a peace.

I was always good at getting hold of any dirty goods now I'm getting hold of Jesus.

God has brought me so far I can't believe it sometimes I shake my head at God's grace and mercy. It's Profound! *Deeeeeeeeeeeeeeeeeeeeeeeeeeeeeep "Boomer"*

Encouragement to each and everyone, we gots to keep hope alive everyone of you that has a criminal record it's not the end of the world.

When I got arrested and acquired a criminal record I saw this thing have an effect on my life. In my fast pace life, I went from one extreme to the next!

To apply for a job was especially a task. When I always used to come to the bit of the application form where it had: do you have a criminal record I remember going through the first sets of application forms putting yes then diverted the answer to a lie then lies upon lies was made up, and still no job my peace of mind from then on was distorted. So back to crime it was 'nope' I had to reject crime! And be persistent focused on having faith. So stop worrying that you will keep taking the wrong road coz "good news brothers and sisters don't loose hope God Has come through for me and He can come through for you".

If your heart and your focus is right He will provide and make a way where there seem to be no way. Even you will find jobs you won't have to answer yes or no as to whether you a have criminal record or not.

Coz God promotes you and gives you a new life. God Is Your Source

SALVATION GAVE ME LIFE

I swallowed my pride and sought for help from an experienced person on how to fill out applications and compile a CV, which helped. People can help you in life, there are always people around to help and who may even give you a job!

Talking about careers, rappers, singers, actors that finally get their fame and money are still unsatisfied, they got all that money but still unhappy, still insecure, still paranoid, still no peace! Yoga, drugs, alcohol, a partner, drugs can't save you! You pay a price for everything in this life one of the things you pay for when you get fame is your peace, liberty and freedom.

People get false impressions about these so-called stars but if you knew what they were going through you would be shocked. The majority of them are unsatisfied and unhappy!

We try to justify everything, how long we think we will live and all that jazz, your destiny is not in your own hands it's in God's hands when you live for Him. Your destiny is important, don't let the devil have access to it! God is real and can't nobody do me like Jesus!

FOCUS I need a favour! Please just "TEST" GOD!

Want out! Try Him Jesus and see the result! Since I lived fully for Christ my relationship with my parents is good the joke is they used to get on my nerves.

Life is all about learning, life is what you make it!

Finding a breakthrough from God in times of need is what you want and what you need. Stop the ducking and diving trying to avoid God not everyone makes it out of sin, if you don't you will die and go to hell. So walk in FAVOUR! Favour, Favour, Favour do you want Favour! God will give it you!

To my biological sisters Sade, Jumoke, Moji, I love you, my biological brothers Michael, Femi, cousins Kemi, Ilene, Glen Jamel, Pearl, Evangelist Jackson, God daughters Kalesha, Tashana, my entire family and friends Ben, Daniel, Leone, Amanda, Lorraine, Matthew, Darrel, Nigel, Kessa, the Chantel's, Menelik, Glen, Carl, Eddy, Wendy, David, Sachel, Wayne. I love you all and want to see you all succeed and spread the word of righteousness. Ps Sade I don't wanna see any boyfriends sniffing around until you're at least *18!*

I was fortunate to have both parents there. To those of you that had a single parent or foster parent *Keep Ya Head Up!*

We Have To Change Everyday For The Good. We Need To Be Prepared For Change Everyday We Can't Remain The Same!

Remember: What you become is what you do with the promises of God!

I learnt that from Bible School from a Blessed Pastor called Carlton Williams.

Did you catch that!

What you become is what you do with the promises of God!

Luke Chapter 8 Verse 11 – 15

Chapter 28

SUMMARY

There's just too much to say. I could have gone on, and on, and on, and on, and on and, on, but I would never have been able to finish this book!

I really enjoyed writing this book it wasn't easy I can't even spell properly and I'm not good with punctuation. *"I just got used" "straight up and down, what a blessing in itself!* Something tried to stop it from *happening*! *Naturally* we all know the hinderer! My computer broke down on me twice causing me to lose half my book twice! Plus crucial parts and points I wanted to get across!

It was the Holy Spirit writing the book not me so the Holy Spirit led me again!

At this point in time I am writing this book I am living right to the best I know how, living by the Word not making up my own rules, mind you I used to do a lot of that.

On the 6th November 2001 I just started on this book. As I was using the computer on this day in my room, it crossed my mind this computer is not even paid for yet and the money is due December 2001 so I had to tell myself *"I'm keeping up tha faith in God to help me."*

Adding to this bit now is deep coz I did not touch this book since march 2002 until now January, February 2003 coz I was shaken for a while due to the tragedy that took place in my life at the time, explained in **Chapter 13** of this book. The deep thing is God did help me pay *£1,700* it was faith and a blessing God just came through for me. How? God provided a job so I worked *"everybody has to work brethren! "You feel me". 'Seek' 'First' God's kingdom and His 'Righteousness' and all will be added unto you.*

I want you to know everything that was taking place whilst I was getting this book ready that's why I wrote it.

So that's why I didn't hold back coz I'm telling it like it is, whether anybody likes it or not!

It's all about tha truth! It sets you free.........words are powerful!!!!

"For me personally brethren, I've always thought big! I never was afraid to go anywhere or do anything. I'm not asking you to do anything, but you are accountable for what you know, you need to follow the guidelines and will for your life!

The Bible (God's Mind) Jesus is real, heaven is real. "Word is born" what's the use a man gaining the whole world yet lose his soul? Deep proverb, parable, riddle, example! Deeeeeeeeeeeeeeeecccceeep!

God used me to write this book I had to get this book out by any means necessary. I went down the (self publishing route) coz I wanted to express myself as myself totally. So I could relate to my generation. It was hard work coz I stayed up very late many nights seeing the darkness of the evening then suddenly the light of the morning editing the book, entering corrections and all that jazz. It paid off in the end though. And this goes to show you anything is possible, you have the ability to achieve anything in this temporary life, if I can do this anyone can.

I didn't sit down worrying how or when I could write and get this book out there.

I just did it!

Everything I have said in this book is all undiluted truth! Everything!

All I have shared have all been my personal experiences.

This book has been a confirmation of God's Word and plans, I have been amazed by the proof and confirmation, that I was meant to actually write this book for such a time as this!

My steps are truly ordered by G-O-D! When you feel you need to step out and do something, overcome and let the blessing unfold, you are ABLE, you are more than a conqueror, the joy of tha Lord is your strength.

We are led by the Spirit, if we want to be! "At the end of the day" we have to let faith and God do their work, just go with the flow of the things of God and put your whole trust in Him! I am encouraging and stirring you up, by my experiences!

The pastor at the church I used to attend said to me once: *'Grace'* and *'Mercy'* is available for today! Don't worry about tomorrow, the grace and mercy may not be available tomorrow.

It's true man, words are powerful God created them, don't glorify sickness and problems, stop right there, wake up and recognise and realise your authority and power! Not everyone catches things straight away or is quick to act, just the *"will"* the willingness is what carries you. We forget sometimes things are only for a season, plus we forget we need to be on guard at all times, meaning spiritually, prayed up, keeping in the Word (The Bible). We need to keep hearing encouragement and words from the Bible (God's Mind) over and over again.

It needs to sink in and saturate our entire body, soul and Spirit, forget about all this premeditated stuff, yoga, chanting, witchcraft, telling you to empty out your mind, the question is empty it out for what? Not for good! So be careful, be real with yourself and God you ain't a saint we all are sinners.

I ain't proud of all the bad things I have done, but I have learnt from my past and I'm now using it for God's glory!

"I'll let you in on a secret I got to read and finish a book "The unquenchable worshiper" by Matt Redman.

12pm 09/04/2003 I finished reading my first book, I actually read it all. What an achievement, it would have been *"liberties"* if I had not finished that Matt Redman book, coz I got given it twice as a present from Susan Reid a good friend, I lost the book and she bought it again! So it would have been a major conviction if I neglected that book!

That book is *"brilly"* I strongly recommend "The unquenchable worshiper".

I did try to read the Vinne Jones auto bio but I didn't get that far; it's all good though!

How did I write the book? I wrote it on my computer, and spell check helped me alot, but most of all the wisdom from God, the Holy Spirit!

I aimed to encourage the Christian people out there, more importantly the people labelled as criminals, prisoners, thugs, gangsters, the dying world and the unsaved, rejected people, people who don't know God, "Jesus to Christ"

I enjoyed being myself talking street, being inspired by the Holy Spirit of God especially for all the street peoples on road to relate, identify and communicate keeping it real like the King James version of the Holy Bible! The amplified version of the Bible breaks it down though. *You get me! Seen!*

"Okay I close with tha last encouragement", don't say I never told you, coz God is not complicated, and you are now accountable for what you know.

I laid all my cards on the table: *"you know"*: The stealing, women I slept with, the ten cars I had without having a driver's licence, fake IDs, drunk states of mind, robbery, hot wiring cars, bad habits, etcetera, etcetera. it's your turn to gain focus and be an encouragement and give your life to God Almighty, Jesus to Christ!

Before you leave this book please take the opportunity to give your life to God! Remember it has to be from your heart and you have got to mean it!

Don't let the devil steal your joy or intimidate you to make you feel you are nuts! *This is personal!* Grab your *salvation* and be *saved! Forever!*

"No one said it would be easy at first".

Chapter 29

Invitation

Salvation Prayer

Get a Bible and turn to **Romans chapter 10 verse 9**

It says: *if you confess with your mouth the Lord Jesus and believe in your heart that God has raised Him from the dead, you will be saved.*

Jesus Christ is able to do exceedingly abundantly above all you can ever imagine in your life!

"Repeat these words: *Lord Jesus, I realise I am a sinner I realise I am not complete without you, come into my heart Lord Jesus, I confess you are my Lord, Saviour and God, come into my life and my heart right now, I accept you as my Lord and I receive the gift of the Holy Spirit and Salvation through your infinite Grace by FAITH! Amen (So be it!)*

Simple Prayer Guidelines To Read:

The Lord is my Shepherd: Psalm Chapter 23

Our Father: Matthew chapter 6 verse 9

No matter if you're Black White, Brown, Yellow, Pink, Red, Burgundy, God loves you and wants you to be right. He wants you to be reconciled with Him, if you don't know what that is check it out in a dictionary I did!

I have learnt you keep learning, nobody is perfect, I also learned the way my parents brought me up, was the best, they knew how! However I would do it differently with my kids!

All things that start, start from a small thing then it gets bigger, whatever the situation or need, prayer, habits to be broken, work needed, addictions, I took you on a brief journey on what I did, when I did it, how I did it! How I overcome and conquered it!

The aim of the game of getting this book out to you was to heal and set people free! Knowing that we all go through similar things and nobody is perfect.

I didn't think it would take me three years to complete this book. I had to be reprogrammed, from habits and lifestyles and I can now open up!

Now I see life, situations and things for what they really are.

The Bible (God's Mind) says: The things we see are temporal, but the things we do not see are eternal. Which is without a shadow of a doubt true!

Money, power, fame, or sex, won't bring you happiness, only God. *"Only God my friend.*

As you can see I'm not perfect! We all have faults.

I have always wanted to hear five words 'I am proud of you' from my parents but if I don't hear it, I know God is proud of me!

"We all are ministers we just need to activate our gift".

The truth is what I'm bringing, I can tell you so much, but the essence is the *"truth sets you free"* and you know the truth now! You decide what you do with the key. "You Choose"........................

Life Or Death?

My life was AMAZE, SIN then GRACE.....................

LIFE: in a sense of heaven and peace, DEATH: in a sense of not accepting God and living in sin!

This is my story, it's all about making moves the right ones! If I can do it you definitely can, it won't happen over night, it's a process who knows though it could? Only God knows!

"I Know, that I know, that I know you will find that peace in Jesus trust me! Your Zeal for peace will pay off!

As I said before when you're done reading this book, you need to apply the Word of God to your life, if you want effective change coz nothing will change until you apply the Word of God to your life.

Shalom (Peace).

Please read the whole book and chapters of:

<u>Matthew</u> - <u>Revelation</u> chapter 1 – End (and get your own revelation, insight and eye-opener from God)

You must constantly study the Word of God you can't figure it out in a day it is a process, I repeat, say again, replicate, reiterate it is a process!

Agape behaviour!

"God Bless you" signing out!

: A voice of one crying out in the wilderness

By Evangelist Teslim Johnson x

God's Promises

Romans chapter 10 verse 9. John chapter 3 verse 16.

John chapter 15 verse 15. Hebrews chapter 11 verse 1.

Psalms chapter 91 verse 1. Psalms chapter 118 verse 8.

Galatians chapter 5 verse 22. Philippians Chapter 3 verse 13.

Philippians chapter 4 verse 19. Ephesians chapter 1 verse 3.

Acts chapter 1 verse 8. Deuteronomy chapter 28 Verse 13.

Daniel chapter 11 verse 32.

Recommended Books

Ian Christensen 'You Can Develop Strong Faith'
(ISBN1-903725-11-9)

Matt Redman 'Unquenchable Worshipper'
(ISBN 0-85476-995-1)

Tony Anthony 'Taming The Tiger'
(ISBN 1-86024-481-5)

Dez Brown with Martin Saunders 'Convicted Or Condemned'
(ISBN 1-86024-484-X)

John Ankerberg & John Weldon
The Facts On Islam (ISBN 0-7369-1107-3)
The Facts On Jehovah's Witnesses (ISBN 0-7369-1108-1)
The Facts On Why You Can Believe The Bible
The Facts On The Mormon Church
The Facts On Homosexuality

Agape Behaviour Publishing 2005

To Keith,
Much Love
Agape Behaviour

Romans 8v28